THE

BRICKS 'N BLOOMS

BEAUTIFUL & EASY-CARE

FLOWER
GARDEN
PLANNER

STACY LING

TEN PEAKS PRESS®
EUGENE, OR

Contents

Introduction

How to Use This Planner

Welcome to *The Bricks 'n Blooms Beautiful and Easy-Care Flower Garden Planner.* This book will help you bring your flower garden to life through planning, journaling, and referencing while giving you an easy way to keep track of your progress. You'll create a mood board, set design goals, and bring those designs to life while keeping track of the seeds you plant, the flowers you grow, their bloom times, and their performance in your garden.

As a gardener who's been growing flowers for well over 25 years, I can honestly say I don't remember much about prior growing seasons unless I write it down. Sure, I generally remember things like, *Oh, that coreopsis was really beautiful in the cottage garden.* But the variety of coreopsis, when it bloomed, and how it ended up doing? If I didn't write it down, I can't remember it.

The funny thing is, every year I tell myself, *You'll remember the name of that plant* (as I repeat it 20 times to myself). But you know what? I never do! Year after year, I ask myself questions like: *What was the variety of that coreopsis again? When did I plant those snapdragons and pinch them back? How long did it take the zinnias to start blooming after I planted the seedlings?*

For years, I kept a small notebook filled with bits and pieces about my gardens. But it wasn't well-organized, and it was hard to follow the random, incomplete thoughts I'd jotted down.

When cell phones became more like minicomputers, I started keeping better notes in my phone, but they were never organized, consistent, or easy to follow and reference.

It was hard to find the information I needed when I needed it, because it wasn't all written down in one place. For example, I tried to grow foxgloves for a number of years, but I never wrote down when or where I planted them—or even when and how they declined. I thought I'd remember because, hey, I'm a gardener—but I didn't! (Those foxgloves never returned, by the way.) Writing down key information would have helped me figure out why they had failed so I could fix the problem and grow foxgloves with greater success the following season.

The lack of a good journaling system can be a major detriment when you want to successfully design, plant, and grow a beautiful flower garden over time in a manageable way. *Do you absolutely need a record-keeping system?* No. I've gotten by for most of my gardening life without one. But it's really helpful to record your journey so you develop a good understanding of what works and what doesn't. Because ultimately, it will help you plan, learn, and grow as a gardener—and it will make things a lot easier for you.

After writing *The Bricks 'n Blooms Guide to a Beautiful and Easy-Care Flower Garden*, I pulled all that information together to develop this user-friendly guide to designing, planting, and growing flower gardens in an organized, manageable way. I created a place where I can quickly reference information, remember details, and keep track of all things related to my gardens. I wrote down how certain plants adapted to my soil, noted their growing conditions, and kept track of how they performed.

Instead of trying to remember every zinnia variety I grew from seed to flower by frantically searching for the sales receipt in my inbox, I use this planner to keep a record of everything I purchased so I can quickly look it up when it's time to order seeds each year. I also won't need to track down the seed packets for sowing information, because I can quickly look at my journal to see when I need to start them each year.

Keeping a record of what you planted, when you planted it, how it performed, and what you'd do differently in the future is invaluable for growing a low-maintenance flower garden that blooms year after year. Instead of trying to grow plants that never seem to thrive, you'll learn what plants do well in your garden so you can focus on growing more of those.

But this book is so much more than just a planning and journaling tool. I also included all my best gardening tips—all in one handy resource—to help you design, plan, and create the flower garden of your dreams.

Your green thumb starts ... now! Let's get growing!

Tips for Using This Garden Planner

- Use it to help you create a mood board for your garden. This will help you pull a cohesive and attractive look together that represents your own personal garden style.

- Plan your flower garden layout and design, brainstorm planting ideas, and create a plant wish list—all based on the measurements and details of every garden space.

- Use it as a reference tool for quick design tips, ideal plant combinations, practical—and attractive—garden designs, and more.

- Keep track of weather and climate information so you can learn how the weather and potential severe conditions in your area impact your garden. Learn from your mistakes! If your cosmos were toppled by a strong breeze, staking them next season will prevent a repeat performance. Mophead hydrangeas with beautiful, big blooms can be vulnerable to winter chills. Protecting them with burlap or other coverings can ensure those flower buds survive harsh winters. If you notice your peony blooms flopping over to the ground, add some grow-through hoops as they break ground so they are better supported when they bloom.

- Record your successes and failures in your planner so you can learn what works and what doesn't in your garden.

- Use the planner as a daily garden diary where you write down what you love and don't love about your garden, planting or sowing dates, bloom times, seasonal observations, any pest and disease problems your garden experiences, or anything else. Write down whether you want to grow certain plants again or where you might want to move plants around in your garden.

- Create an heirloom keepsake where you, your children, your grandchildren, or even future stewards of your garden can discover the history of your garden, learn from your experience, and grow and care for their own outdoor areas.

At the end of the day, I want the process of growing flowers to be easy for you. I want you to enjoy yourself and keep gardening! You might be looking at all the charts and worksheets in this planner and wondering what you've gotten yourself into. Please don't feel overwhelmed—they're just tools to help get you going on the path to flower-gardening success. Use what works for you and your gardening endeavors this season; you'll get a feel for what makes sense as you go. You may or may not use it all, and that's okay!

Keep this planner handy so you'll see it every day and remember to use it. Make it a part of your routine—the more you use it, the greater the benefit you'll receive in the long run. By taking the time to journal and record details, you'll learn how to grow things from your own experiences. And really, that's the best way to learn.

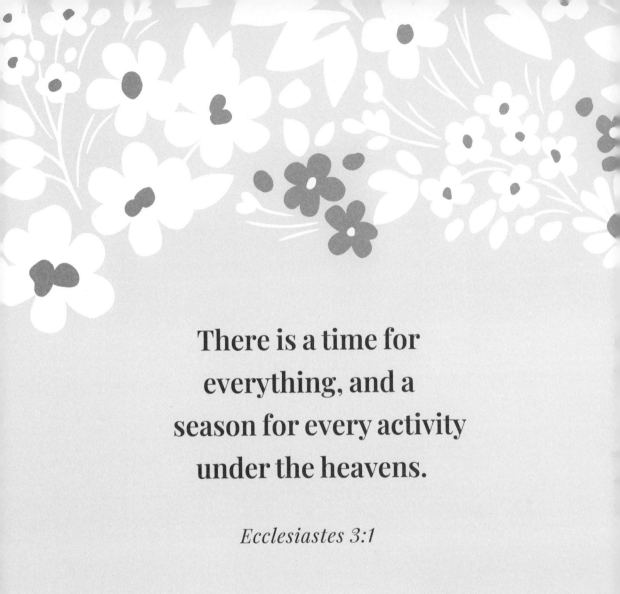

There is a time for
everything, and a
season for every activity
under the heavens.

Ecclesiastes 3:1

Flowers appear
on the earth;
the season of singing
has come.

Song of Songs 2:12

Part One

Understanding Your Garden

Before you start growing plants, it's important to learn the basics about your garden, your growing conditions, and how much space you have available to grow things. In this section, we're covering your specific growing conditions and reviewing plants and tools you already have, so you can create a plan for your future garden. When you understand more about your own space, you can design a garden that works for you, choose the right plants for your area, and start planting for success.

About Your
HARDINESS ZONE

It's very important to become familiar with your climate before purchasing plants and growing a garden. Not all plants will thrive in all hardiness zones, and certain perennial plants—which tend to be more expensive—may not return the next year because they are not hardy to that zone.

NOT SURE WHAT
HARDINESS ZONE YOU'RE IN?

You can check here:
planthardiness.ars.usda.gov

Learn Your First and Last Frost Date

Your hardiness zone will guide you to the first and last frost date for your microclimate. A frost date is the average date of the first and last light freeze in spring and fall for a particular zone. And that first and last frost date is significant because it tells you what you can plant and when.

Typically, your local nursery will carry plants and flowers that can be grown in your specific microclimate. Just understand the differences between what is annual and what is perennial in your hardiness zone (see chapters 4 and 5 of *The Bricks 'n Blooms Guide to a Beautiful and Easy-Care Flower Garden* for more on this). If you are unsure, ask the nursery staff, check with an experienced gardening friend, or reach out to your local cooperative extension.

If you order seeds or starts from a plant catalog, read the description well so you know what can be grown successfully in your zone.

YOUR GARDENING ZONE AND FIRST AND LAST FROST DATE:

My Gardening Zone is:_____

My Average Last Frost Date is:_____ My Average First Frost Date is:_____

About Your
SOIL

Understanding your soil quality is integral for gardening success, so a little bit of knowledge goes a long way. In this section we'll record soil characteristics, soil test results (if taken), drainage, and the size and shape of your garden. Keep in mind that different gardens in your landscape may have different types of soil, so wherever you are growing things, take notes on the soil in that area.

Your Soil's Characteristics

TEXTURE: ☐ Sandy   ☐ Clay   ☐ Loamy   ☐ Silty

HOW WELL MY GARDEN DRAINS: _____

_____

SOIL TEST RESULTS:

If you had your soil tested (and I hope you did), record the results here for easy reference.

Soil Nutrient Levels: _____

_____

_____

Results: _____

_____

_____

Recommendations: _____

_____

_____

ADDED SOIL AMENDMENTS

Did you make the recommended adjustments or add compost, leaf mold, and composted manure? Record it here.

DATE ADDED	SOIL AMENDMENT

DATE ADDED	SOIL AMENDMENT

Your Garden
SIZE

Total Lot Size (The Big Picture)

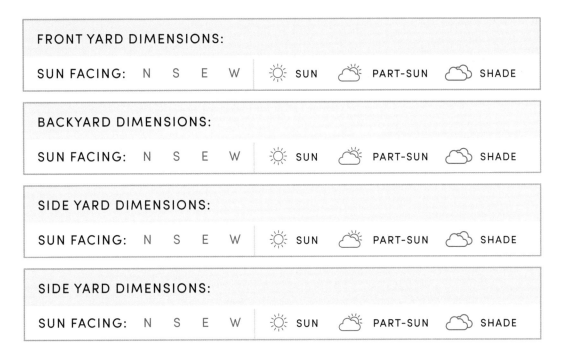

FRONT YARD DIMENSIONS:

SUN FACING: N   S   E   W | ☀ SUN   ⛅ PART-SUN   ☁ SHADE

BACKYARD DIMENSIONS:

SUN FACING: N   S   E   W | ☀ SUN   ⛅ PART-SUN   ☁ SHADE

SIDE YARD DIMENSIONS:

SUN FACING: N   S   E   W | ☀ SUN   ⛅ PART-SUN   ☁ SHADE

SIDE YARD DIMENSIONS:

SUN FACING: N   S   E   W | ☀ SUN   ⛅ PART-SUN   ☁ SHADE

Garden Dimensions and Growing Requirements

Measure your garden spaces and determine how much square footage you have for growing. Include measurements for any structures or garden features like a pond, fence, or fountain, and factor everything into your calculations.

Calculating Your
GARDEN SPACES

Research and plan out your garden spaces if you are starting fresh or sprucing up an existing garden. Write everything down about each garden space, including light conditions, soil quality, and drainage, so you can determine which plants are best suited for that area. By planning it out ahead of time, you'll be more directed when you shop and less likely to make impulse purchases. (Or at least you'll significantly cut down on them!)

Garden Space

LENGTH: _____ WIDTH: _____ HEIGHT (IF ANY): _____

SOIL DRAINAGE: _____

LIGHT CONDITIONS: _____

STRUCTURE DIMENSIONS (IF ANY): _____

ADDITIONAL NOTES: _____

_____

_____

_____

_____

_____

Garden Design Layout

Quick Tip! Each box should represent one square foot.

Garden Space

LENGTH: _____ WIDTH: _____ HEIGHT (IF ANY): _____

SOIL DRAINAGE: _____
_____
_____
_____

LIGHT CONDITIONS: _____
_____
_____
_____

STRUCTURE DIMENSIONS (IF ANY): _____
_____
_____
_____

ADDITIONAL NOTES: _____
_____
_____
_____
_____
_____
_____
_____
_____
_____

Garden Space

LENGTH: _____ WIDTH: _____ HEIGHT (IF ANY): _____

SOIL DRAINAGE: _____

_____

_____

_____

LIGHT CONDITIONS: _____

_____

_____

_____

STRUCTURE DIMENSIONS (IF ANY): _____

_____

_____

_____

ADDITIONAL NOTES: _____

_____

_____

_____

_____

_____

_____

_____

Garden Design Layout

Garden Space

LENGTH: _____ WIDTH: _____ HEIGHT (IF ANY): _____

SOIL DRAINAGE: _____

_____

_____

_____

LIGHT CONDITIONS: _____

_____

_____

_____

STRUCTURE DIMENSIONS (IF ANY): _____

_____

_____

_____

ADDITIONAL NOTES: _____

_____

_____

_____

_____

_____

_____

_____

_____

_____

Garden Space

LENGTH: _____ WIDTH: _____ HEIGHT (IF ANY): _____

SOIL DRAINAGE: _____
_____
_____
_____

LIGHT CONDITIONS: _____
_____
_____
_____

STRUCTURE DIMENSIONS (IF ANY): _____
_____
_____
_____

ADDITIONAL NOTES: _____
_____
_____
_____
_____
_____
_____
_____
_____
_____

Taking Inventory of What You're
ALREADY GROWING

If you have an existing garden, use the following worksheets to inventory plants you are currently growing, the variety of those plants (if known) and their needs (such as soil type and light and water requirements), and note any pest and/or disease problem. This will help you decide whether those plants are worth continuing to grow long term and if they are worth dividing or propagating down the road.

Trees

DATE PLANTED	VARIETY	BLOOM TIME	
CONDITIONS NEEDED		PRUNING/DEADHEADING	PEST/DISEASE

DATE PLANTED	VARIETY	BLOOM TIME	
CONDITIONS NEEDED		PRUNING/DEADHEADING	PEST/DISEASE

DATE PLANTED	VARIETY	BLOOM TIME	
CONDITIONS NEEDED		PRUNING/DEADHEADING	PEST/DISEASE

DATE PLANTED	VARIETY	BLOOM TIME
CONDITIONS NEEDED	PRUNING/DEADHEADING	PEST/DISEASE

DATE PLANTED	VARIETY	BLOOM TIME
CONDITIONS NEEDED	PRUNING/DEADHEADING	PEST/DISEASE

DATE PLANTED	VARIETY	BLOOM TIME
CONDITIONS NEEDED	PRUNING/DEADHEADING	PEST/DISEASE

DATE PLANTED	VARIETY	BLOOM TIME
CONDITIONS NEEDED	PRUNING/DEADHEADING	PEST/DISEASE

DATE PLANTED	VARIETY	BLOOM TIME
CONDITIONS NEEDED	PRUNING/DEADHEADING	PEST/DISEASE

DATE PLANTED	VARIETY	BLOOM TIME	
CONDITIONS NEEDED		PRUNING/DEADHEADING	PEST/DISEASE

DATE PLANTED	VARIETY	BLOOM TIME	
CONDITIONS NEEDED		PRUNING/DEADHEADING	PEST/DISEASE

DATE PLANTED	VARIETY	BLOOM TIME	
CONDITIONS NEEDED		PRUNING/DEADHEADING	PEST/DISEASE

DATE PLANTED	VARIETY	BLOOM TIME	
CONDITIONS NEEDED		PRUNING/DEADHEADING	PEST/DISEASE

DATE PLANTED	VARIETY	BLOOM TIME	
CONDITIONS NEEDED		PRUNING/DEADHEADING	PEST/DISEASE

DATE PLANTED	VARIETY	BLOOM TIME
CONDITIONS NEEDED	PRUNING/DEADHEADING	PEST/DISEASE

DATE PLANTED	VARIETY	BLOOM TIME
CONDITIONS NEEDED	PRUNING/DEADHEADING	PEST/DISEASE

DATE PLANTED	VARIETY	BLOOM TIME
CONDITIONS NEEDED	PRUNING/DEADHEADING	PEST/DISEASE

DATE PLANTED	VARIETY	BLOOM TIME
CONDITIONS NEEDED	PRUNING/DEADHEADING	PEST/DISEASE

DATE PLANTED	VARIETY	BLOOM TIME
CONDITIONS NEEDED	PRUNING/DEADHEADING	PEST/DISEASE

Perennials

DATE PLANTED	VARIETY	BLOOM TIME	
CONDITIONS NEEDED		PRUNING/DEADHEADING	PEST/DISEASE

DATE PLANTED	VARIETY	BLOOM TIME	
CONDITIONS NEEDED		PRUNING/DEADHEADING	PEST/DISEASE

DATE PLANTED	VARIETY	BLOOM TIME	
CONDITIONS NEEDED		PRUNING/DEADHEADING	PEST/DISEASE

DATE PLANTED	VARIETY	BLOOM TIME	
CONDITIONS NEEDED		PRUNING/DEADHEADING	PEST/DISEASE

DATE PLANTED	VARIETY	BLOOM TIME	
CONDITIONS NEEDED		PRUNING/DEADHEADING	PEST/DISEASE

Perennials

DATE PLANTED	VARIETY	BLOOM TIME	
CONDITIONS NEEDED		PRUNING/DEADHEADING	PEST/DISEASE

DATE PLANTED	VARIETY	BLOOM TIME	
CONDITIONS NEEDED		PRUNING/DEADHEADING	PEST/DISEASE

DATE PLANTED	VARIETY	BLOOM TIME	
CONDITIONS NEEDED		PRUNING/DEADHEADING	PEST/DISEASE

DATE PLANTED	VARIETY	BLOOM TIME	
CONDITIONS NEEDED		PRUNING/DEADHEADING	PEST/DISEASE

DATE PLANTED	VARIETY	BLOOM TIME	
CONDITIONS NEEDED		PRUNING/DEADHEADING	PEST/DISEASE

Annuals

DATE PLANTED	VARIETY	BLOOM TIME	
CONDITIONS NEEDED		PRUNING/DEADHEADING	PEST/DISEASE

DATE PLANTED	VARIETY	BLOOM TIME	
CONDITIONS NEEDED		PRUNING/DEADHEADING	PEST/DISEASE

DATE PLANTED	VARIETY	BLOOM TIME	
CONDITIONS NEEDED		PRUNING/DEADHEADING	PEST/DISEASE

DATE PLANTED	VARIETY	BLOOM TIME	
CONDITIONS NEEDED		PRUNING/DEADHEADING	PEST/DISEASE

DATE PLANTED	VARIETY	BLOOM TIME	
CONDITIONS NEEDED		PRUNING/DEADHEADING	PEST/DISEASE

DATE PLANTED	VARIETY	BLOOM TIME	
CONDITIONS NEEDED		PRUNING/DEADHEADING	PEST/DISEASE

DATE PLANTED	VARIETY	BLOOM TIME	
CONDITIONS NEEDED		PRUNING/DEADHEADING	PEST/DISEASE

DATE PLANTED	VARIETY	BLOOM TIME	
CONDITIONS NEEDED		PRUNING/DEADHEADING	PEST/DISEASE

DATE PLANTED	VARIETY	BLOOM TIME	
CONDITIONS NEEDED		PRUNING/DEADHEADING	PEST/DISEASE

DATE PLANTED	VARIETY	BLOOM TIME	
CONDITIONS NEEDED		PRUNING/DEADHEADING	PEST/DISEASE

Spring-Flowering Bulbs

DATE PLANTED	VARIETY	BLOOM TIME	
CONDITIONS NEEDED		PRUNING/DEADHEADING	PEST/DISEASE

DATE PLANTED	VARIETY	BLOOM TIME	
CONDITIONS NEEDED		PRUNING/DEADHEADING	PEST/DISEASE

DATE PLANTED	VARIETY	BLOOM TIME	
CONDITIONS NEEDED		PRUNING/DEADHEADING	PEST/DISEASE

DATE PLANTED	VARIETY	BLOOM TIME	
CONDITIONS NEEDED		PRUNING/DEADHEADING	PEST/DISEASE

DATE PLANTED	VARIETY	BLOOM TIME	
CONDITIONS NEEDED		PRUNING/DEADHEADING	PEST/DISEASE

Spring-Flowering Bulbs

DATE PLANTED	VARIETY	BLOOM TIME	
CONDITIONS NEEDED		PRUNING/DEADHEADING	PEST/DISEASE

DATE PLANTED	VARIETY	BLOOM TIME	
CONDITIONS NEEDED		PRUNING/DEADHEADING	PEST/DISEASE

DATE PLANTED	VARIETY	BLOOM TIME	
CONDITIONS NEEDED		PRUNING/DEADHEADING	PEST/DISEASE

DATE PLANTED	VARIETY	BLOOM TIME	
CONDITIONS NEEDED		PRUNING/DEADHEADING	PEST/DISEASE

DATE PLANTED	VARIETY	BLOOM TIME	
CONDITIONS NEEDED		PRUNING/DEADHEADING	PEST/DISEASE

Ground Covers

DATE PLANTED	VARIETY	BLOOM TIME	
CONDITIONS NEEDED		PRUNING/DEADHEADING	PEST/DISEASE

DATE PLANTED	VARIETY	BLOOM TIME	
CONDITIONS NEEDED		PRUNING/DEADHEADING	PEST/DISEASE

DATE PLANTED	VARIETY	BLOOM TIME	
CONDITIONS NEEDED		PRUNING/DEADHEADING	PEST/DISEASE

DATE PLANTED	VARIETY	BLOOM TIME	
CONDITIONS NEEDED		PRUNING/DEADHEADING	PEST/DISEASE

DATE PLANTED	VARIETY	BLOOM TIME	
CONDITIONS NEEDED		PRUNING/DEADHEADING	PEST/DISEASE

DATE PLANTED	VARIETY	BLOOM TIME	
CONDITIONS NEEDED		PRUNING/DEADHEADING	PEST/DISEASE

DATE PLANTED	VARIETY	BLOOM TIME	
CONDITIONS NEEDED		PRUNING/DEADHEADING	PEST/DISEASE

DATE PLANTED	VARIETY	BLOOM TIME	
CONDITIONS NEEDED		PRUNING/DEADHEADING	PEST/DISEASE

DATE PLANTED	VARIETY	BLOOM TIME	
CONDITIONS NEEDED		PRUNING/DEADHEADING	PEST/DISEASE

DATE PLANTED	VARIETY	BLOOM TIME	
CONDITIONS NEEDED		PRUNING/DEADHEADING	PEST/DISEASE

She considers a field and
buys it; out of her earnings
she plants a vineyard.
She sets about her work
vigorously; her arms are
strong for her tasks.

Proverbs 31:16-17

Part Two

Designing and Planning

In this section, we're designing and planning the garden for the upcoming growing season. This is the place where you'll dream, plan, reference, prepare, and record. You'll find some quick planning, designing, growing, and planting references with tips, and you can peruse several predesigned gardens to fit different goals or special needs. Plus, you'll have a workspace where you can plan your own designs and keep track of what plants or seeds you need to acquire to make those dreams a reality.

Garden Design
BASICS

- Consider your garden location so you can group together plants with the same light and watering requirements.

- Conceptualize your garden design by making a mood board or creating a folder of flowers and designs you love.

- Think about bloom time, colors, textures, flowers, and foliage shapes.

- Create mixed borders with bulbs, annuals, perennials, shrubs, and evergreens.

- Plant according to spacing and height, with shorter plants in front and taller plants in back.

- Include a focal point like a fountain, obelisk, or birdhouse.

- Consider critter issues before planting. Deer, rabbits, groundhogs, and other wildlife all like to munch on plants.

- Determine if you will need to add fencing or figure out another way to deter critters from your garden.

- Plant in odd numbers for an aesthetically pleasing design.

- Repeat the same plants and colors throughout your design so the garden flows and your eye is drawn fluidly throughout the bed.

Creating a
MOOD BOARD

If you're not sure where to begin, create a mood board for your garden that will capture the desired look and feel you want in your outdoor space. This is a great way to gather inspiration, experiment with different ideas, and communicate your vision to anyone involved in helping you create your dream garden.

Here's what you can include in your mood board:

- **Images of gardens you love:** Find pictures of gardens that resonate with you, whether it's a specific style like cottage or Japanese Zen, a particular color palette, or the use of certain features like an arbor, statue, birdbath, or obelisk. You can find inspiration by paging through magazines, browsing online resources like Pinterest, or even walking around your own neighborhood!

- **Plant choices:** Gather pictures of the flowers, shrubs, and trees you want to include in your garden. Consider factors like bloom time, foliage color and texture, and a plant's ability to attract pollinators or create privacy.

- **Hardscaping elements:** Include pictures of pathways, patios, decks, fences, water features, or any other structural elements you envision in your garden. Think about the materials you like, such as wood, stone, brick, or concrete.

- **Furniture and accessories:** Add pictures of outdoor furniture, lighting, planters, sculptures, or anything else that will add personality, character, and functionality to your space.

- **Color swatches and textures:** Don't forget about the overall feel you want to create in your garden. Include paint chips, fabric samples, or even natural materials like pebbles or wood chips to represent the textures and colors you'd like to incorporate.

Once you've gathered your inspiration, arrange it on a physical board (like cork or foam) or create a digital version using software like Canva or Photoshop. Experiment and adjust your mood board as you go. The most important thing is that it reflects your unique vision for your garden.

Helpful Tips

- **Focus on your lifestyle:** Think about how you'll use your garden and choose elements that cater to your needs and preferences. Do you love to entertain? Include a dining area and string lights. Do you want to raise your garden off the ground so it's easier to work? Raised beds are a great solution. Want to keep the bugs away from an outdoor living space? Consider planting flowers that help repel mosquitos.

- **Consider your climate:** Choose plants and materials that are best suited to your hardiness zone, light, and soil conditions.

- **Be creative:** There are no rules when it comes to creating a mood board! Use your imagination and have fun with it. You're not committed to the designs and colors you choose—a mood board just gets you going with your gardening dreams.

Deer-Resistant Garden
DESIGNS

Quick Tips for Deer-Resistant Gardening

While no method is foolproof, there are a few precautions you can take to deter deer from your garden—or at least minimize the amount of damage they can do to your plants.

- Plant smart. Consult the Rutgers Cooperative Extension list to see various plants, trees, and shrubs rated by level of deer resistance.

- Use combination plantings. When planting higher risk plants, group them with plants that are at less risk of being nibbled by deer.

- Spray susceptible plants with deer repellent, such as Deer Out.

- Install fencing that is at least eight feet high.

- Use scare tactic devices with motion sensors to frighten deer out of your yard.

- Get a dog.

- Walk your gardens daily to observe for signs of browsing.

- Prepare in early spring so you are ready to deal with deer damage before it gets out of control.

PLANTS WITH HIGHER DEER RESISTANCE			
Agastache	Salvia	Statice	Strawflower
Bleeding heart	Globe thistle	Marigold	Rosemary
Russian sage	Iris	Cleome	Daffodil
False indigo	Snapdragon	Forget-me-not	Peony
Larkspur	Allium	Lamb's ear	Oregano
Nepeta	Lavender	Ligularia	Flowering tobacco

Deer-Resistant Garden Design Ideas

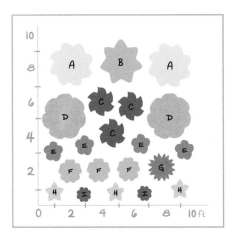

COLORFUL FULL-SUN GARDEN

A — Monarda

B — Russian sage 'Denim 'n Lace'

C — Cleome

D — Echinops

E — Allium 'Globemaster'

F — Bearded iris

G — Nepeta 'Walker's Low'

H — Sweet alyssum

I — Lantana

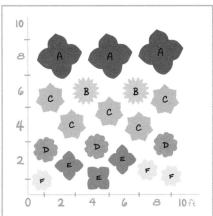

SHADE/PART-SHADE GARDEN

A — Ligularia 'Bottle Rocket'

B — Bleeding heart

C — Astilbe

D — Hellebore

E — Lungwort

F — Epimedium

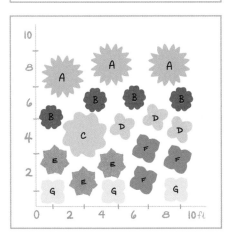

PURPLE FULL-SUN GARDEN

A — Baptisia

B — Allium 'Globemaster'

C — Monarda

D — Bearded iris

E — Lavender 'Hidcote'

F — Salvia 'May Night'

G — Lamb's ear

Everblooming Flower Garden
DESIGNS

Quick Tips for an Everblooming Flower Garden

- Choose wisely. Research plant hardiness, light needs, and the mature size of each plant. Opt for low-maintenance varieties for an easy-care garden.

- Plant for all seasons. Include spring bulbs along with perennials, shrubs, and evergreens for year-round color and interest. Use annuals to fill in gaps in the various blooming times.

- Deadhead and maintain your plants. Regularly remove spent blooms to encourage new growth. Keep your garden tidy with weeding, mulching, and watering for optimal plant health and continuous flowering.

EVERBLOOMING QUICK LIST

—— SPRING ——		—— SUMMER ——		—— FALL ——
Tulip	Salvia	Echinacea	Coreopsis	Aster
Daffodil	Knockout rose	Rudbeckia	Joe Pye weed	Chrysanthemum
Allium	Peony	Bee balm	Hydrangea	Winter pansy
Iris	Hydrangea	Butterfly weed	Tall garden phlox	Ornamental grass
Creeping phlox	Lenten rose	Daylily	Dahlia	Beautyberry
Catmint		Liatris		

Everblooming Flower Garden Design Ideas

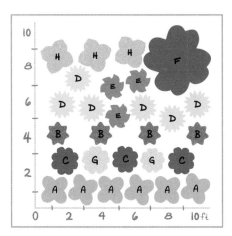

FULL-SUN GARDEN

A — Tulips
B — Daffodils
C — Nepeta
D — Coneflower
E — Rudbeckia
F — Hydrangea
G — Sedum 'Autumn Joy'
H — Agastache

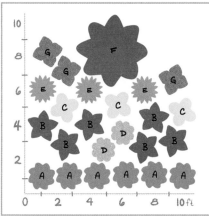

SHADE GARDEN

A — Impatiens
B — Hellebores
C — Bleeding hearts
D — Brunnera
E — Hostas
F — Rhododendron
G — Goatsbeard

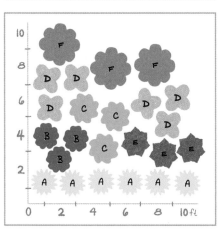

FOUR-SEASON COLOR GARDEN

A — Petunias
B — Salvia
C — Coreopsis
D — Coneflower
E — Sedum 'Autumn Joy'
F — Boxwood

Cottage Garden
DESIGNS

Quick Tips for Growing a Cottage Garden

- Start with a small garden and expand it as you gain experience.

- Begin with structural plants like small evergreens and flowering shrubs and trees.

- Add a focal point to plant around, such as a birdbath, birdhouse, arbor, bench, chair, fence, path, or other hardscaping element.

- Plant flowers in groupings with lots of color, texture, dimension, and different bloom times.

- Repeat plant types and colors for a natural visual flow throughout the bed.

	Lavender	Sedum 'Autumn Joy'	Pansy
COTTAGE	Iris	Daylily	Forget-me-not
GARDEN	Echinacea	Hydrangea	Marigold
FLOWERS	Peony	Daisy	Sunflower
	Rudbeckia	Snapdragon	...and so much more

Cottage Garden Design Ideas

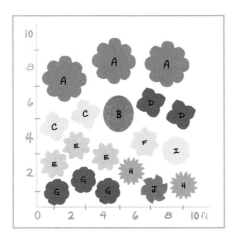

SPRING

A — Baptisia

B — Birdbath

C — Siberian iris

D — Penstemon

E — Salvia 'May Night'

F — Nepeta 'Walker's Low'

G — Myosotis (forget-me-not)

H — Dianthus

I — Peony

J — Pansy

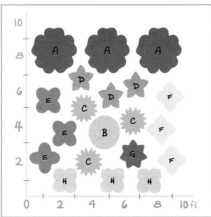

SUMMER

A — Russian sage 'Denim 'n Lace'

B — Birdhouse

C — Clematis 'Jackmanii'

D — Shasta daisy

E — Echinacea

F — Rudbeckia

G — Nepeta 'Walker's Low'

H — 'Supertunia Vista Bubblegum'

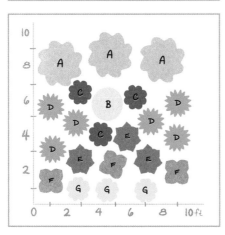

FALL

A — Eupatorium (Joe Pye weed)

B — Obelisk (two feet wide)

C — Sweet autumn clematis (to climb the obelisk)

D — Japanese anenome

E — Sedum 'Autumn Joy'

F — Aster

G — Pansy

Butterfly Garden DESIGNS

Designing a Pollinator Garden

Butterflies and hummingbirds flitting from flower to flower are fun to watch, and they are essential partners that help ensure a thriving, vibrant garden. These fascinating creatures act as pollinators, carrying pollen between plants, leading to increased production of fruits, vegetables, and of course, even more flowers. We can plant our gardens to entice them to our landscape.

Quick Tips for Designing a Butterfly Garden

- Butterflies favor native plants. Look up which plants are native to your area— and focus on those that attract butterflies.

- Avoid pesticides in your garden because they can harm butterflies and other pollinators.

- Butterflies are drawn to brightly colored purples, blues, yellows, whites, and pinks.

- Plant a succession of flowers that bloom spring through fall to keep butterflies returning to your garden.

- Butterflies are attracted to clusters of like colors, so plant groupings of flowers.

- Focus on plants with multiple florets and composite flowers because they allow butterflies to get more nectar. Avoid double-flowering varieties because they carry less nectar.

PLANTS THAT ATTRACT BUTTERFLIES			
	Butterfly weed	Sedum 'Autumn Joy'	Bee balm
	Agastache	Zinnia	Blazing star
	Purple coneflower	Joe Pye weed	

Butterfly Garden Design Ideas

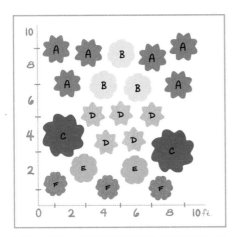

COLORFUL GARDEN

A — Agastache
B — Coneflower
C — Tall Phlox
D — Liatris
E — Nepeta
F — Coreopsis

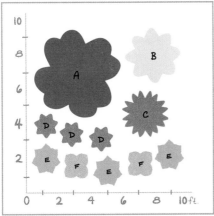

PINK GARDEN

A — Weigela 'Wine and Roses'
B — Eupatorium (Joe Pye weed)
C — Monarda
D — Zinnia 'Benary's Giant Wine'
E — Sedum 'Autumn Joy'
F — Dianthus

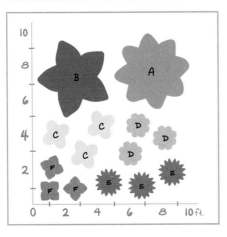

BLUE/PURPLE GARDEN

A — Lilac 'Bloomerang'
B — Rose of Sharon 'Purple Pillar'
C — Agastache
D — Coneflower
E — Salvia 'May Night'
F — Hemerocallis 'Purple De Oro'

Hummingbird Garden
DESIGNS

Quick Tips for Designing a Hummingbird Garden

Designing a garden that attracts hummingbirds is very similar to designing a butterfly garden, with some slight nuances.

- Plant a variety of flowers and shrubs in varying heights to provide hummingbirds with shade, shelter, food, and water.

- Hummingbirds love brightly colored, tubular flowers because they hold more nectar—and the shape makes it easy for the hummingbirds to get the nectar out of them. Hummingbirds are also drawn to red, orange, pink, and yellow hues.

- Attract hummingbirds to your garden with early blooming varieties so they start visiting your garden at the beginning of the season.

- Grow similar flowers together in large groupings so hummingbirds can spot them more easily while flying.

PLANTS THAT ATTRACT HUMMINGBIRDS			
	Nepeta	Cleome	Petunia
	Bee balm	Columbine	Hibiscus
	Purple coneflower	Impatiens	Weigela hosta

Hummingbird Garden Design Ideas

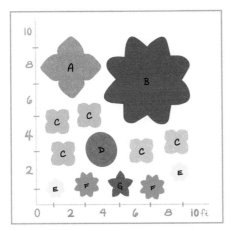

COLORFUL GARDEN

A — Monarda
B — Hardy hibiscus
C — Coneflower
D — Birdbath
E — Daylily
F — Nepeta
G — Petunia

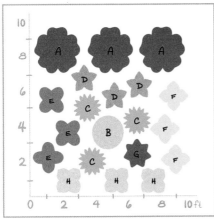

PINK GARDEN

A — Weigela 'Wine and Roses'
B — Monarda
C — Salvia 'Pink Profusion'
D — Coneflower
E — Cleome
F — 'Supertunia Vista Bubblegum'
G — Achillea 'Firefly Amethyst'

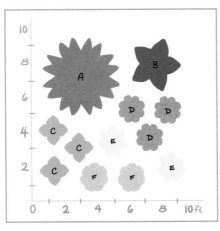

BLUE/PURPLE GARDEN

A — Lilac 'Bloomerang'
B — Caryopteris 'Longwood Blue'
C — Salvia 'May Night'
D — Agastache 'Blue Fortune'
E — Nepeta 'Walker's Low'
F — 'Supertunia Latte'

Plants That
LOOK GOOD TOGETHER

Annuals

SHADE/PART SHADE | Coleus, sweet potato vine, and double flowering impatiens

PART SHADE | Coleus, bacopa, sweet potato vine, and begonia

FULL SUN | Geranium, baby's-breath euphorbia, petunia, and bacopa

FULL SUN | Marigold, baby's-breath euphorbia, petunia, and lantana

FULL SUN | Zinnia, snapdragon, and petunia

SUN, FALL FLOWERING | Chrysanthemum, pansy, and celosia

SUN, SPRING FLOWERING | Pansy, ranunculus, and licorice plant

Perennials

SHADE | Hosta, astilbe, and hellebore

PART SHADE/SHADE | Brunnera, hellebore, and Virginia bluebell

SHADE WITH ANNUALS | Bleeding heart, hosta, astilbe, lungwort, and impatiens

SUN | Echinacea, monarda, Russian sage, Joe Pye weed, and sedum 'Autumn Joy'

SUN | Coreopsis, achillea, echinacea, salvia, and nepeta

SUN | Baptisia, monarda, Russian sage, coneflower, rudbeckia, coreopsis, and lavender

SUN WITH ANNUALS | Baptisia, Russian sage, coneflower, rudbeckia, zinnia, and petunia

Spring-flowering bulbs

SUN | Tulip, daffodil, and allium

SUN | Crocus, grape hyacinth, and tulip

SUN | Grape hyacinth, tulip, and daffodil

SUN WITH PERENNIALS AND ANNUALS | Allium, coneflower, nepeta, salvia, creeping phlox, myosotis, tulip, and pansy

SUN WITH PERENNIALS AND ANNUALS | Allium, baptisia, snapdragon, peony, nepeta, creeping phlox, tulip, daffodil, and pansy

PARTIAL SHADE WITH PERENNIALS AND ANNUALS | Bleeding heart, Virginia bluebell, brunnera, hellebore, Spanish bluebell, hyacinth, and crocus

Shrubs

PART SUN | Ninebark, hydrangea, and viburnum

PART SUN | Abelia, weigela, and spirea

FULL SUN | Limelight hydrangea, purple smoketree, and callicarpa

FULL SUN | Ninebark, limelight hydrangea, and caryopteris

SHADE | Rhododendron, azalea, and andromeda

SHADE | Rhododendron, bottlebrush buckeye, and mountain laurel

Plant
WISH LIST

PLANT NAME	QTY	WHERE & WHEN TO BUY
DESCRIPTION		
		DATE ACQUIRED

PLANT NAME	QTY	WHERE & WHEN TO BUY
DESCRIPTION		
		DATE ACQUIRED

PLANT NAME	QTY	WHERE & WHEN TO BUY
DESCRIPTION		
		DATE ACQUIRED

PLANT NAME	QTY	WHERE & WHEN TO BUY
DESCRIPTION		
		DATE ACQUIRED

PLANT NAME	QTY	WHERE & WHEN TO BUY
DESCRIPTION		
		DATE ACQUIRED

PLANT NAME	QTY	WHERE & WHEN TO BUY
DESCRIPTION		
		DATE ACQUIRED

PLANT NAME	QTY	WHERE & WHEN TO BUY
DESCRIPTION		
		DATE ACQUIRED

PLANT NAME	QTY	WHERE & WHEN TO BUY
DESCRIPTION		
		DATE ACQUIRED

PLANT NAME	QTY	WHERE & WHEN TO BUY
DESCRIPTION		
		DATE ACQUIRED

PLANT NAME	QTY	WHERE & WHEN TO BUY
DESCRIPTION		
		DATE ACQUIRED

PLANT NAME	QTY	WHERE & WHEN TO BUY
DESCRIPTION		
		DATE ACQUIRED

PLANT NAME	QTY	WHERE & WHEN TO BUY
DESCRIPTION		
		DATE ACQUIRED

PLANT NAME	QTY	WHERE & WHEN TO BUY
DESCRIPTION		
		DATE ACQUIRED

PLANT NAME	QTY	WHERE & WHEN TO BUY
DESCRIPTION		
		DATE ACQUIRED

PLANT NAME	QTY	WHERE & WHEN TO BUY
DESCRIPTION		
		DATE ACQUIRED

PLANT NAME	QTY	WHERE & WHEN TO BUY
DESCRIPTION		
		DATE ACQUIRED

PLANT NAME	QTY	WHERE & WHEN TO BUY
DESCRIPTION		
		DATE ACQUIRED

PLANT NAME	QTY	WHERE & WHEN TO BUY
DESCRIPTION		
		DATE ACQUIRED

PLANT NAME	QTY	WHERE & WHEN TO BUY
DESCRIPTION		
		DATE ACQUIRED

Calculating Your
GARDEN AREA

When you're designing your garden, it's a good idea to calculate how much space you have so you know how many plants to buy. This will help you avoid overbuying, it will cut down on impulse purchases, and it will give you more direction. Here's how to calculate your garden area.

1. Measure the area with a tape measure to determine the length and width of your garden.

2. Calculate the area by multiplying the length by the width to get the total square footage.

3. Use plant tags or an online description to determine the recommended spacing between plants based on the size they will reach at maturity.

4. Divide the total square footage of the garden by the recommended spacing between plants to determine the maximum number of plants that can fit in the area.

5. Depending on the shape of your garden, you may need to round up or down to account for any gaps or spaces between plants. I lean toward rounding up. I'd rather have too many plants than not enough.

How to Calculate Your Seed Order

- Measure the area of your garden to determine the total square footage.

- Check the seed packet for the recommended planting distance between each seed. This will help you determine how many plants you can fit in your garden area.

- Seeds don't always germinate, so it's best to buy extra to make up for any that don't sprout. Buy 10 to 20 percent more than you think you will need.

- Consider the size of harvest you'd like to have—large or small.

Seed
INVENTORY

Use this list to keep track of what you have and what you buy. Many seeds are good for two to four years before they lose their viability, if stored in a cool and dry place.

BUY DATE	FLOWER VARIETY	QTY	SOURCE	BUY MORE?	YEAR
				Y N	
				Y N	
				Y N	
				Y N	
				Y N	
				Y N	
				Y N	
				Y N	
				Y N	
				Y N	

BUY DATE	FLOWER VARIETY	QTY	SOURCE	BUY MORE?	YEAR
				Y N	
				Y N	
				Y N	
				Y N	
				Y N	
				Y N	
				Y N	
				Y N	
				Y N	
				Y N	
				Y N	
				Y N	
				Y N	
				Y N	
				Y N	

BUY DATE	FLOWER VARIETY	QTY	SOURCE	BUY MORE?	YEAR
				Y N	
				Y N	
				Y N	
				Y N	
				Y N	
				Y N	
				Y N	
				Y N	
				Y N	
				Y N	
				Y N	
				Y N	
				Y N	
				Y N	
				Y N	

Let us go early to the
vineyards to see if the vines
have budded, if their blossoms
have opened, and if the
pomegranates are in bloom.

Song of Songs 7:12

Part Three

Planting
and Growing

Now that we've covered the basics and found our inspiration, it's time to plant and grow a flower garden! Here, you'll embark on your flower-growing adventure, from planting and sowing techniques to seed-starting schedules, with handy worksheets that'll guide you through each step and act as a quick reference.

How to
PLANT A GARDEN

1. Lay out your plants in the garden area. Space the plants accordingly. (It will be less work for you later!)

2. Using a shovel or hand trowel, dig a hole two times the size of the root ball for each plant.

3. Remove the plant from the plastic nursery pot, fanning the roots out with your fingers to encourage them to grow outside the root ball. If plants are rootbound, use a shovel or sharp knife to slice through the roots first, then fan the roots out with your fingers to loosen them. This won't damage the plant, helps the roots grow out into the soil, and improves plant health.

4. Add fresh garden soil with amendments to the hole before planting.

5. Set the new plant in the hole, making sure the plant's soil surface lines up with the ground's soil surface.

6. Backfill the hole with fresh garden soil, amendments, and existing soil.

7. Top the bed off with fresh mulch.

8. Water well.

Starting Seeds for Your
CUT FLOWER GARDEN

If you want to start a cut flower garden this year, it is best to start it from seed.

You can start seeds indoors under grow lights or sow them outdoors.

INDOOR SEED-STARTING SUPPLY LIST

☐ Seeds   ☐ Drainage trays   ☐ Heat mat

☐ Shelf system or table   ☐ Oscillating fan   ☐ Plant labels

☐ Vermiculite   ☐ Grow lights   ☐ Programmable Timer

☐ Clear dome lids   ☐ Seed-starting soil   ☐ Watering can

☐ Pots or cell trays

How to Sow
SEEDS INDOORS

1. Premoisten the seed-starting soil in a separate tray or bucket.

2. Fill and pack down the soil in each cell or pot to remove air pockets.

3. Sow seeds according to the directions (typically planting them two times their depth).

4. Drop 1 to 2 seeds into each hole, then cover the holes with vermiculite. While you can also cover them with soil, vermiculite is easier for the seeds to grow through.

5. Label each cell, tray, and pot because you won't remember the varieties later.

6. Cover the pots or trays with a clear plastic dome or similar covering.

7. Many seeds germinate quicker on heat mats under grow lights. Use a timer and set the grow lights to be on for 14 to 16 hours per day.

8. Watch for seed germination every day. Some varieties will take a few days, while others will take longer.

9. When seedlings emerge, remove the plastic covering and take them off the heat mats, even if they didn't all sprout, because more will germinate later.

10. Maintain seedlings under grow lights about an inch or so away from the tallest seedling. You'll need to adjust the lights as the seedlings grow.

11. Check the soil daily to make sure it stays evenly moist. Always water from the bottom so you don't damage fragile seedlings with overhead watering. If you start seeds with a water reservoir, you can just keep the reservoir filled. You can also set trays and pots in a pan filled with water for roughly an hour per day.

12. As seedlings grow, reread the seed packets to see if there are any special instructions to follow, like pinching back the growing seedlings.

13. Use an oscillating fan set on low to promote air circulation.

14. Rotate trays or pots every so often to encourage seedlings to grow upright instead of leaning in one direction to reach the light.

15. About two weeks before your last frost date, start hardening off seedlings.

Timeline for Cut Flower Garden
SEED STARTING INDOORS

When you look through the many seeds available to grow in your cut flower garden, it can feel overwhelming. Here is a general timeline of my favorite cut flowers to grow that are easy to germinate and grow from seed to flower. Different seed varieties from different growers may vary, but this chart will give you a general framework for planning. Always read the seed packet for specific sowing instructions. To get your dates, refer to your last frost date on page 13.

FLOWER	INDOOR SOW DATE *(weeks before last frost)*	DIRECT SOW? *(after last frost)*	WINTER SOW?	MY SOW DATE
SWEET PEA	10 to 12	no	yes	
SNAPDRAGON	8 to 10	no	yes	
LARKSPUR	8 to 10	no	yes	
GOMPHRENA	6 to 8	no	no	
COSMOS	5 to 7	yes	no	
AMARANTH	4 to 6	yes	no	
CELOSIA	4 to 6	yes	no	
STRAWFLOWER	4 to 6	yes	no	
ZINNIA	4	yes	no	

FLOWER	INDOOR SOW DATE (weeks before last frost)	DIRECT SOW? (after last frost)	WINTER SOW?	MY SOW DATE
BORAGE	none	yes	no	
CALENDULA	none	yes	yes	
NASTURTIUM	none	yes	no	
SUNFLOWER	none	yes	no	
TITHONIA	none	yes	no	

Seed-Starting
SCHEDULE & RECORD

Most cut flowers thrive with at least six to eight hours of direct sunlight daily. Research the sizes of your desired flowers and see how much sunny space you have available in your garden. You can even grow a cut flower garden in planters if you're short on space!

NOT SURE WHAT KIND OF LIGHT YOU HAVE?

After the trees leaf out in the spring, observe different areas of your yard throughout the day to find the sunniest spot.

Use the following worksheets to help you plan your seed-sowing schedule and track the progress of your seedlings. Don't forget to label each cell and tray well! If you start any seeds indoors, make sure you harden them off gradually.

Take copious notes and track sowing dates, plant behavior, and each variety's specific needs as your flowers grow. This information will be invaluable next year, and you'll have all of this information for quick reference when you need it.

Seed-Starting Schedule

MY LAST FROST DATE: _____   4 WEEKS BEFORE: _____

6 WEEKS BEFORE: _____   8 WEEKS BEFORE: _____

10 WEEKS BEFORE: _____   12 WEEKS BEFORE: _____

SOW DATE	PLANT VARIETY	HEIGHT	COLOR
SOWING INFORMATION			HOW MANY SOWED?

SOW DATE	PLANT VARIETY	HEIGHT	COLOR
SOWING INFORMATION			HOW MANY SOWED?

SOW DATE	PLANT VARIETY	HEIGHT	COLOR
SOWING INFORMATION			HOW MANY SOWED?

SOW DATE	PLANT VARIETY	HEIGHT	COLOR
SOWING INFORMATION			HOW MANY SOWED?

SOW DATE	PLANT VARIETY	HEIGHT	COLOR
SOWING INFORMATION			HOW MANY SOWED?

SOW DATE	PLANT VARIETY	HEIGHT	COLOR
SOWING INFORMATION		HOW MANY SOWED?	

SOW DATE	PLANT VARIETY	HEIGHT	COLOR
SOWING INFORMATION		HOW MANY SOWED?	

SOW DATE	PLANT VARIETY	HEIGHT	COLOR
SOWING INFORMATION		HOW MANY SOWED?	

SOW DATE	PLANT VARIETY	HEIGHT	COLOR
SOWING INFORMATION		HOW MANY SOWED?	

SOW DATE	PLANT VARIETY	HEIGHT	COLOR
SOWING INFORMATION		HOW MANY SOWED?	

SOW DATE	PLANT VARIETY	HEIGHT	COLOR
SOWING INFORMATION		HOW MANY SOWED?	

SOW DATE	PLANT VARIETY	HEIGHT	COLOR
SOWING INFORMATION		HOW MANY SOWED?	

SOW DATE	PLANT VARIETY	HEIGHT	COLOR
SOWING INFORMATION		HOW MANY SOWED?	

SOW DATE	PLANT VARIETY	HEIGHT	COLOR
SOWING INFORMATION		HOW MANY SOWED?	

SOW DATE	PLANT VARIETY	HEIGHT	COLOR
SOWING INFORMATION		HOW MANY SOWED?	

SOW DATE	PLANT VARIETY	HEIGHT	COLOR
SOWING INFORMATION			HOW MANY SOWED?

SOW DATE	PLANT VARIETY	HEIGHT	COLOR
SOWING INFORMATION			HOW MANY SOWED?

SOW DATE	PLANT VARIETY	HEIGHT	COLOR
SOWING INFORMATION			HOW MANY SOWED?

SOW DATE	PLANT VARIETY	HEIGHT	COLOR
SOWING INFORMATION			HOW MANY SOWED?

SOW DATE	PLANT VARIETY	HEIGHT	COLOR
SOWING INFORMATION			HOW MANY SOWED?

SOW DATE	PLANT VARIETY	HEIGHT	COLOR

SOWING INFORMATION	HOW MANY SOWED?

SOW DATE	PLANT VARIETY	HEIGHT	COLOR

SOWING INFORMATION	HOW MANY SOWED?

SOW DATE	PLANT VARIETY	HEIGHT	COLOR

SOWING INFORMATION	HOW MANY SOWED?

SOW DATE	PLANT VARIETY	HEIGHT	COLOR

SOWING INFORMATION	HOW MANY SOWED?

SOW DATE	PLANT VARIETY	HEIGHT	COLOR

SOWING INFORMATION	HOW MANY SOWED?

Individual
PLANT CARDS

These individual plant cards, tucked neatly into your garden planner, provide a vital snapshot of each resident. With a quick glance, you'll have access to all the information you need to keep your plants thriving, from watering needs and sunlight preferences to ideal planting times and potential pest problems.

1

COMMON NAME:

BOTANICAL NAME:

PLANT VARIETY:

DATE PLANTED:

BLOOM SEASON/COLOR:

DATE HARVESTED:

- ☐ BULB
- ☐ TREE
- ☐ GRASS
- ☐ EVERGREEN
- ☐ SHRUB
- ☐ FLOWER
- ☐ GROUNDCOVER
- ☐ VINE
- ☐ BERRY
- ☐ ANNUAL
- ☐ PERENNIAL
- ☐ TRANSPLANT
- ☐ BIENNIAL
- ☐ SEED

PURCHASE INFORMATION

VENDOR:

COST: QTY:

WATERING SCHEDULE

SUNLIGHT EXPOSURE

SOIL REQUIREMENTS

- ☐ ACID
- ☐ ALKALINE

CARE INSTRUCTIONS:

PLANT WORTHINESS:

INSECT/DISEASE PROBLEMS:

FERTILIZER/TREATMENTS:

ADDITIONAL NOTES:

2

COMMON NAME: BOTANICAL NAME:

PLANT VARIETY: DATE PLANTED:

BLOOM SEASON/COLOR: DATE HARVESTED:

- ☐ BULB
- ☐ EVERGREEN
- ☐ GROUNDCOVER
- ☐ ANNUAL
- ☐ BIENNIAL
- ☐ TREE
- ☐ SHRUB
- ☐ VINE
- ☐ PERENNIAL
- ☐ SEED
- ☐ GRASS
- ☐ FLOWER
- ☐ BERRY
- ☐ TRANSPLANT

PURCHASE INFORMATION

VENDOR:

COST: QTY:

WATERING SCHEDULE ◌ ◌ ◌

SUNLIGHT EXPOSURE ☼ ☼ ☼

SOIL REQUIREMENTS

☐ ACID

☐ ALKALINE

CARE INSTRUCTIONS:

PLANT WORTHINESS:

FERTILIZER/TREATMENTS:

INSECT/DISEASE PROBLEMS:

ADDITIONAL NOTES:

3

COMMON NAME: BOTANICAL NAME:

PLANT VARIETY: DATE PLANTED:

BLOOM SEASON/COLOR: DATE HARVESTED:

- [ ] BULB
- [ ] EVERGREEN
- [ ] GROUNDCOVER
- [ ] ANNUAL
- [ ] BIENNIAL
- [ ] TREE
- [ ] SHRUB
- [ ] VINE
- [ ] PERENNIAL
- [ ] SEED
- [ ] GRASS
- [ ] FLOWER
- [ ] BERRY
- [ ] TRANSPLANT

PURCHASE INFORMATION

VENDOR:

COST: QTY:

WATERING SCHEDULE

SUNLIGHT EXPOSURE

SOIL REQUIREMENTS
- [ ] ACID
- [ ] ALKALINE

CARE INSTRUCTIONS:

PLANT WORTHINESS:

FERTILIZER/TREATMENTS:

INSECT/DISEASE PROBLEMS:

ADDITIONAL NOTES:

4

COMMON NAME: BOTANICAL NAME:

PLANT VARIETY: DATE PLANTED:

BLOOM SEASON/COLOR: DATE HARVESTED:

- [ ] BULB
- [ ] EVERGREEN
- [ ] GROUNDCOVER
- [ ] ANNUAL
- [ ] BIENNIAL
- [ ] TREE
- [ ] SHRUB
- [ ] VINE
- [ ] PERENNIAL
- [ ] SEED
- [ ] GRASS
- [ ] FLOWER
- [ ] BERRY
- [ ] TRANSPLANT

PURCHASE INFORMATION

VENDOR:

COST: QTY:

WATERING SCHEDULE   ◊ ◊ ◊

SUNLIGHT EXPOSURE   ☼ ☼ ☼

SOIL REQUIREMENTS
- [ ] ACID
- [ ] ALKALINE

CARE INSTRUCTIONS:

PLANT WORTHINESS:

FERTILIZER/TREATMENTS:

INSECT/DISEASE PROBLEMS:

ADDITIONAL NOTES:

5

COMMON NAME:

BOTANICAL NAME:

PLANT VARIETY:

DATE PLANTED:

BLOOM SEASON/COLOR:

DATE HARVESTED:

- [ ] BULB
- [ ] TREE
- [ ] GRASS
- [ ] EVERGREEN
- [ ] SHRUB
- [ ] FLOWER
- [ ] GROUNDCOVER
- [ ] VINE
- [ ] BERRY
- [ ] ANNUAL
- [ ] PERENNIAL
- [ ] TRANSPLANT
- [ ] BIENNIAL
- [ ] SEED

PURCHASE INFORMATION

VENDOR:

COST: QTY:

WATERING SCHEDULE

SUNLIGHT EXPOSURE

SOIL REQUIREMENTS
- [ ] ACID
- [ ] ALKALINE

CARE INSTRUCTIONS:

PLANT WORTHINESS:

FERTILIZER/TREATMENTS:

INSECT/DISEASE PROBLEMS:

ADDITIONAL NOTES:

6

COMMON NAME: BOTANICAL NAME:

PLANT VARIETY: DATE PLANTED:

BLOOM SEASON/COLOR: DATE HARVESTED:

- [ ] BULB
- [ ] TREE
- [ ] GRASS

- [ ] EVERGREEN
- [ ] SHRUB
- [ ] FLOWER

- [ ] GROUNDCOVER
- [ ] VINE
- [ ] BERRY

- [ ] ANNUAL
- [ ] PERENNIAL
- [ ] TRANSPLANT

- [ ] BIENNIAL
- [ ] SEED

PURCHASE INFORMATION

VENDOR:

COST: QTY:

WATERING SCHEDULE

SUNLIGHT EXPOSURE

SOIL REQUIREMENTS

- [ ] ACID
- [ ] ALKALINE

CARE INSTRUCTIONS:

PLANT WORTHINESS:

FERTILIZER/TREATMENTS:

INSECT/DISEASE PROBLEMS:

ADDITIONAL NOTES:

COMMON NAME: BOTANICAL NAME:

PLANT VARIETY: DATE PLANTED:

BLOOM SEASON/COLOR: DATE HARVESTED:

- ☐ BULB   ☐ EVERGREEN   ☐ GROUNDCOVER   ☐ ANNUAL   ☐ BIENNIAL
- ☐ TREE   ☐ SHRUB   ☐ VINE   ☐ PERENNIAL   ☐ SEED
- ☐ GRASS   ☐ FLOWER   ☐ BERRY   ☐ TRANSPLANT

PURCHASE INFORMATION

VENDOR:

COST: QTY:

WATERING SCHEDULE

SUNLIGHT EXPOSURE

SOIL REQUIREMENTS

☐ ACID

☐ ALKALINE

CARE INSTRUCTIONS:

PLANT WORTHINESS:

FERTILIZER/TREATMENTS:

INSECT/DISEASE PROBLEMS:

ADDITIONAL NOTES:

8

COMMON NAME: BOTANICAL NAME:

PLANT VARIETY:

DATE PLANTED:

BLOOM SEASON/COLOR:

DATE HARVESTED:

- [ ] BULB
- [ ] EVERGREEN
- [ ] GROUNDCOVER
- [ ] ANNUAL
- [ ] BIENNIAL
- [ ] TREE
- [ ] SHRUB
- [ ] VINE
- [ ] PERENNIAL
- [ ] SEED
- [ ] GRASS
- [ ] FLOWER
- [ ] BERRY
- [ ] TRANSPLANT

PURCHASE INFORMATION

VENDOR:

COST: QTY:

WATERING SCHEDULE

SUNLIGHT EXPOSURE

SOIL REQUIREMENTS

- [ ] ACID
- [ ] ALKALINE

CARE INSTRUCTIONS:

PLANT WORTHINESS:

FERTILIZER/TREATMENTS:

INSECT/DISEASE PROBLEMS:

ADDITIONAL NOTES:

9

COMMON NAME: BOTANICAL NAME:

PLANT VARIETY:

DATE PLANTED:

BLOOM SEASON/COLOR:

DATE HARVESTED:

- ☐ BULB
- ☐ EVERGREEN
- ☐ GROUNDCOVER
- ☐ ANNUAL
- ☐ BIENNIAL
- ☐ TREE
- ☐ SHRUB
- ☐ VINE
- ☐ PERENNIAL
- ☐ SEED
- ☐ GRASS
- ☐ FLOWER
- ☐ BERRY
- ☐ TRANSPLANT

PURCHASE INFORMATION

VENDOR:

COST: QTY:

WATERING SCHEDULE   💧 💧 💧

SUNLIGHT EXPOSURE   ☀ ☀ ☀

SOIL REQUIREMENTS

- ☐ ACID
- ☐ ALKALINE

CARE INSTRUCTIONS:

PLANT WORTHINESS:

FERTILIZER/TREATMENTS:

INSECT/DISEASE PROBLEMS:

ADDITIONAL NOTES:

COMMON NAME:

BOTANICAL NAME:

PLANT VARIETY:

DATE PLANTED:

BLOOM SEASON/COLOR:

DATE HARVESTED:

- [ ] BULB
- [ ] TREE
- [ ] GRASS
- [ ] EVERGREEN
- [ ] SHRUB
- [ ] FLOWER
- [ ] GROUNDCOVER
- [ ] VINE
- [ ] BERRY
- [ ] ANNUAL
- [ ] PERENNIAL
- [ ] TRANSPLANT
- [ ] BIENNIAL
- [ ] SEED

PURCHASE INFORMATION

VENDOR:

COST: QTY:

WATERING SCHEDULE

SUNLIGHT EXPOSURE

SOIL REQUIREMENTS

- [ ] ACID
- [ ] ALKALINE

CARE INSTRUCTIONS:

PLANT WORTHINESS:

FERTILIZER/TREATMENTS:

INSECT/DISEASE PROBLEMS:

ADDITIONAL NOTES:

COMMON NAME:

BOTANICAL NAME:

PLANT VARIETY:

DATE PLANTED:

BLOOM SEASON/COLOR:

DATE HARVESTED:

- [ ] BULB
- [ ] EVERGREEN
- [ ] GROUNDCOVER
- [ ] ANNUAL
- [ ] BIENNIAL
- [ ] TREE
- [ ] SHRUB
- [ ] VINE
- [ ] PERENNIAL
- [ ] SEED
- [ ] GRASS
- [ ] FLOWER
- [ ] BERRY
- [ ] TRANSPLANT

PURCHASE INFORMATION

VENDOR:

COST: QTY:

WATERING SCHEDULE

SUNLIGHT EXPOSURE

SOIL REQUIREMENTS
- [ ] ACID
- [ ] ALKALINE

CARE INSTRUCTIONS:

PLANT WORTHINESS:

FERTILIZER/TREATMENTS:

INSECT/DISEASE PROBLEMS:

ADDITIONAL NOTES:

12

COMMON NAME: _____   BOTANICAL NAME: _____

PLANT VARIETY: _____

DATE PLANTED: _____

BLOOM SEASON/COLOR: _____

DATE HARVESTED: _____

- ☐ BULB
- ☐ TREE
- ☐ GRASS
- ☐ EVERGREEN
- ☐ SHRUB
- ☐ FLOWER
- ☐ GROUNDCOVER
- ☐ VINE
- ☐ BERRY
- ☐ ANNUAL
- ☐ PERENNIAL
- ☐ TRANSPLANT
- ☐ BIENNIAL
- ☐ SEED

PURCHASE INFORMATION

VENDOR:

COST: QTY:

WATERING SCHEDULE   ◊ ◊ ◊

SUNLIGHT EXPOSURE   ☼ ☼ ☼

SOIL REQUIREMENTS

- ☐ ACID
- ☐ ALKALINE

CARE INSTRUCTIONS:

PLANT WORTHINESS:

FERTILIZER/TREATMENTS:

INSECT/DISEASE PROBLEMS:

ADDITIONAL NOTES:

13

COMMON NAME: BOTANICAL NAME:

PLANT VARIETY: DATE PLANTED:

BLOOM SEASON/COLOR: DATE HARVESTED:

- [ ] BULB
- [ ] EVERGREEN
- [ ] GROUNDCOVER
- [ ] ANNUAL
- [ ] BIENNIAL
- [ ] TREE
- [ ] SHRUB
- [ ] VINE
- [ ] PERENNIAL
- [ ] SEED
- [ ] GRASS
- [ ] FLOWER
- [ ] BERRY
- [ ] TRANSPLANT

PURCHASE INFORMATION

VENDOR:

COST: QTY:

WATERING SCHEDULE

SUNLIGHT EXPOSURE

SOIL REQUIREMENTS

- [ ] ACID
- [ ] ALKALINE

CARE INSTRUCTIONS:

PLANT WORTHINESS:

FERTILIZER/TREATMENTS:

INSECT/DISEASE PROBLEMS:

ADDITIONAL NOTES:

14

COMMON NAME: _____   BOTANICAL NAME: _____

PLANT VARIETY: _____   DATE PLANTED: _____

BLOOM SEASON/COLOR: _____   DATE HARVESTED: _____

- [ ] BULB
- [ ] TREE
- [ ] GRASS

- [ ] EVERGREEN
- [ ] SHRUB
- [ ] FLOWER

- [ ] GROUNDCOVER
- [ ] VINE
- [ ] BERRY

- [ ] ANNUAL
- [ ] PERENNIAL
- [ ] TRANSPLANT

- [ ] BIENNIAL
- [ ] SEED

PURCHASE INFORMATION

VENDOR:

COST: QTY:

WATERING SCHEDULE ◌ ◌ ◌

SUNLIGHT EXPOSURE ☼ ☼ ☼

SOIL REQUIREMENTS

- [ ] ACID
- [ ] ALKALINE

CARE INSTRUCTIONS:

PLANT WORTHINESS:

FERTILIZER/TREATMENTS:

INSECT/DISEASE PROBLEMS:

ADDITIONAL NOTES:

COMMON NAME:

BOTANICAL NAME:

PLANT VARIETY:

DATE PLANTED:

BLOOM SEASON/COLOR:

DATE HARVESTED:

- [ ] BULB
- [ ] EVERGREEN
- [ ] GROUNDCOVER
- [ ] ANNUAL
- [ ] BIENNIAL
- [ ] TREE
- [ ] SHRUB
- [ ] VINE
- [ ] PERENNIAL
- [ ] SEED
- [ ] GRASS
- [ ] FLOWER
- [ ] BERRY
- [ ] TRANSPLANT

PURCHASE INFORMATION

VENDOR:

COST:

QTY:

WATERING SCHEDULE

SUNLIGHT EXPOSURE

SOIL REQUIREMENTS

- [ ] ACID
- [ ] ALKALINE

CARE INSTRUCTIONS:

PLANT WORTHINESS:

FERTILIZER/TREATMENTS:

INSECT/DISEASE PROBLEMS:

ADDITIONAL NOTES:

COMMON NAME: BOTANICAL NAME:

PLANT VARIETY: DATE PLANTED:

BLOOM SEASON/COLOR: DATE HARVESTED:

- [ ] BULB
- [ ] TREE
- [ ] GRASS
- [ ] EVERGREEN
- [ ] SHRUB
- [ ] FLOWER
- [ ] GROUNDCOVER
- [ ] VINE
- [ ] BERRY
- [ ] ANNUAL
- [ ] PERENNIAL
- [ ] TRANSPLANT
- [ ] BIENNIAL
- [ ] SEED

PURCHASE INFORMATION

VENDOR:

COST: QTY:

WATERING SCHEDULE

SUNLIGHT EXPOSURE

SOIL REQUIREMENTS
- [ ] ACID
- [ ] ALKALINE

CARE INSTRUCTIONS:

PLANT WORTHINESS:

FERTILIZER/TREATMENTS:

INSECT/DISEASE PROBLEMS:

ADDITIONAL NOTES:

17

COMMON NAME: _____ BOTANICAL NAME: _____

PLANT VARIETY: _____ DATE PLANTED: _____

BLOOM SEASON/COLOR: _____ DATE HARVESTED: _____

- ☐ BULB
- ☐ TREE
- ☐ GRASS
- ☐ EVERGREEN
- ☐ SHRUB
- ☐ FLOWER
- ☐ GROUNDCOVER
- ☐ VINE
- ☐ BERRY
- ☐ ANNUAL
- ☐ PERENNIAL
- ☐ TRANSPLANT
- ☐ BIENNIAL
- ☐ SEED

PURCHASE INFORMATION	WATERING SCHEDULE	💧 💧 💧	SOIL REQUIREMENTS
VENDOR:			☐ ACID
COST: QTY:	SUNLIGHT EXPOSURE	☀ ☀ ☀	☐ ALKALINE

CARE INSTRUCTIONS:

PLANT WORTHINESS:

FERTILIZER/TREATMENTS:

INSECT/DISEASE PROBLEMS:

ADDITIONAL NOTES:

COMMON NAME: BOTANICAL NAME:

PLANT VARIETY: DATE PLANTED:

BLOOM SEASON/COLOR: DATE HARVESTED:

- ☐ BULB
- ☐ EVERGREEN
- ☐ GROUNDCOVER
- ☐ ANNUAL
- ☐ BIENNIAL
- ☐ TREE
- ☐ SHRUB
- ☐ VINE
- ☐ PERENNIAL
- ☐ SEED
- ☐ GRASS
- ☐ FLOWER
- ☐ BERRY
- ☐ TRANSPLANT

PURCHASE INFORMATION

VENDOR:

COST: QTY:

WATERING SCHEDULE   💧 💧 💧

SUNLIGHT EXPOSURE   ☀ ☀ ☀

SOIL REQUIREMENTS

- ☐ ACID
- ☐ ALKALINE

CARE INSTRUCTIONS:

PLANT WORTHINESS:

FERTILIZER/TREATMENTS:

INSECT/DISEASE PROBLEMS:

ADDITIONAL NOTES:

COMMON NAME:

BOTANICAL NAME:

PLANT VARIETY:

DATE PLANTED:

BLOOM SEASON/COLOR:

DATE HARVESTED:

- [ ] BULB
- [ ] EVERGREEN
- [ ] GROUNDCOVER
- [ ] ANNUAL
- [ ] BIENNIAL
- [ ] TREE
- [ ] SHRUB
- [ ] VINE
- [ ] PERENNIAL
- [ ] SEED
- [ ] GRASS
- [ ] FLOWER
- [ ] BERRY
- [ ] TRANSPLANT

PURCHASE INFORMATION

VENDOR:

COST: QTY:

WATERING SCHEDULE

SUNLIGHT EXPOSURE

SOIL REQUIREMENTS

- [ ] ACID
- [ ] ALKALINE

CARE INSTRUCTIONS:

PLANT WORTHINESS:

FERTILIZER/TREATMENTS:

INSECT/DISEASE PROBLEMS:

ADDITIONAL NOTES:

20

COMMON NAME:

BOTANICAL NAME:

PLANT VARIETY:

DATE PLANTED:

BLOOM SEASON/COLOR:

DATE HARVESTED:

- [ ] BULB
- [ ] TREE
- [ ] GRASS
- [ ] EVERGREEN
- [ ] SHRUB
- [ ] FLOWER
- [ ] GROUNDCOVER
- [ ] VINE
- [ ] BERRY
- [ ] ANNUAL
- [ ] PERENNIAL
- [ ] TRANSPLANT
- [ ] BIENNIAL
- [ ] SEED

PURCHASE INFORMATION

VENDOR:

COST: QTY:

WATERING SCHEDULE

SUNLIGHT EXPOSURE

SOIL REQUIREMENTS
- [ ] ACID
- [ ] ALKALINE

CARE INSTRUCTIONS:

PLANT WORTHINESS:

FERTILIZER/TREATMENTS:

INSECT/DISEASE PROBLEMS:

ADDITIONAL NOTES:

COMMON NAME:

BOTANICAL NAME:

PLANT VARIETY:

DATE PLANTED:

BLOOM SEASON/COLOR:

DATE HARVESTED:

- ☐ BULB
- ☐ EVERGREEN
- ☐ GROUNDCOVER
- ☐ ANNUAL
- ☐ BIENNIAL
- ☐ TREE
- ☐ SHRUB
- ☐ VINE
- ☐ PERENNIAL
- ☐ SEED
- ☐ GRASS
- ☐ FLOWER
- ☐ BERRY
- ☐ TRANSPLANT

PURCHASE INFORMATION

VENDOR:

COST: QTY:

WATERING SCHEDULE

SUNLIGHT EXPOSURE

SOIL REQUIREMENTS

- ☐ ACID
- ☐ ALKALINE

CARE INSTRUCTIONS:

PLANT WORTHINESS:

FERTILIZER/TREATMENTS:

INSECT/DISEASE PROBLEMS:

ADDITIONAL NOTES:

22

COMMON NAME: BOTANICAL NAME:

PLANT VARIETY: DATE PLANTED:

BLOOM SEASON/COLOR: DATE HARVESTED:

- [ ] BULB
- [ ] EVERGREEN
- [ ] GROUNDCOVER
- [ ] ANNUAL
- [ ] BIENNIAL
- [ ] TREE
- [ ] SHRUB
- [ ] VINE
- [ ] PERENNIAL
- [ ] SEED
- [ ] GRASS
- [ ] FLOWER
- [ ] BERRY
- [ ] TRANSPLANT

PURCHASE INFORMATION

VENDOR:

COST: QTY:

WATERING SCHEDULE ○ ○ ○

SUNLIGHT EXPOSURE ☼ ☼ ☼

SOIL REQUIREMENTS
- [ ] ACID
- [ ] ALKALINE

CARE INSTRUCTIONS:

PLANT WORTHINESS:

FERTILIZER/TREATMENTS:

INSECT/DISEASE PROBLEMS:

ADDITIONAL NOTES:

COMMON NAME:

BOTANICAL NAME:

PLANT VARIETY:

DATE PLANTED:

BLOOM SEASON/COLOR:

DATE HARVESTED:

- [ ] BULB
- [ ] EVERGREEN
- [ ] GROUNDCOVER
- [ ] ANNUAL
- [ ] BIENNIAL
- [ ] TREE
- [ ] SHRUB
- [ ] VINE
- [ ] PERENNIAL
- [ ] SEED
- [ ] GRASS
- [ ] FLOWER
- [ ] BERRY
- [ ] TRANSPLANT

PURCHASE INFORMATION

VENDOR:

COST: QTY:

WATERING SCHEDULE

SUNLIGHT EXPOSURE

SOIL REQUIREMENTS

- [ ] ACID
- [ ] ALKALINE

CARE INSTRUCTIONS:

PLANT WORTHINESS:

FERTILIZER/TREATMENTS:

INSECT/DISEASE PROBLEMS:

ADDITIONAL NOTES:

COMMON NAME:

BOTANICAL NAME:

PLANT VARIETY:

DATE PLANTED:

BLOOM SEASON/COLOR:

DATE HARVESTED:

- [ ] BULB
- [ ] EVERGREEN
- [ ] GROUNDCOVER
- [ ] ANNUAL
- [ ] BIENNIAL
- [ ] TREE
- [ ] SHRUB
- [ ] VINE
- [ ] PERENNIAL
- [ ] SEED
- [ ] GRASS
- [ ] FLOWER
- [ ] BERRY
- [ ] TRANSPLANT

PURCHASE INFORMATION

VENDOR:

COST: QTY:

WATERING SCHEDULE

SUNLIGHT EXPOSURE

SOIL REQUIREMENTS

- [ ] ACID
- [ ] ALKALINE

CARE INSTRUCTIONS:

PLANT WORTHINESS:

FERTILIZER/TREATMENTS:

INSECT/DISEASE PROBLEMS:

ADDITIONAL NOTES:

25

COMMON NAME:

BOTANICAL NAME:

PLANT VARIETY:

DATE PLANTED:

BLOOM SEASON/COLOR:

DATE HARVESTED:

- [ ] BULB
- [ ] TREE
- [ ] GRASS
- [ ] EVERGREEN
- [ ] SHRUB
- [ ] FLOWER
- [ ] GROUNDCOVER
- [ ] VINE
- [ ] BERRY
- [ ] ANNUAL
- [ ] PERENNIAL
- [ ] TRANSPLANT
- [ ] BIENNIAL
- [ ] SEED

PURCHASE INFORMATION

VENDOR:

COST: QTY:

WATERING SCHEDULE

SUNLIGHT EXPOSURE

SOIL REQUIREMENTS

- [ ] ACID
- [ ] ALKALINE

CARE INSTRUCTIONS:

PLANT WORTHINESS:

FERTILIZER/TREATMENTS:

INSECT/DISEASE PROBLEMS:

ADDITIONAL NOTES:

26

COMMON NAME: BOTANICAL NAME:

PLANT VARIETY:

BLOOM SEASON/COLOR:

DATE PLANTED:

DATE HARVESTED:

- [ ] BULB
- [ ] TREE
- [ ] GRASS
- [ ] EVERGREEN
- [ ] SHRUB
- [ ] FLOWER
- [ ] GROUNDCOVER
- [ ] VINE
- [ ] BERRY
- [ ] ANNUAL
- [ ] PERENNIAL
- [ ] TRANSPLANT
- [ ] BIENNIAL
- [ ] SEED

PURCHASE INFORMATION

VENDOR:

COST: QTY:

WATERING SCHEDULE

SUNLIGHT EXPOSURE

SOIL REQUIREMENTS
- [ ] ACID
- [ ] ALKALINE

CARE INSTRUCTIONS:

PLANT WORTHINESS:

FERTILIZER/TREATMENTS:

INSECT/DISEASE PROBLEMS:

ADDITIONAL NOTES:

COMMON NAME:

BOTANICAL NAME:

PLANT VARIETY:

DATE PLANTED:

BLOOM SEASON/COLOR:

DATE HARVESTED:

- [ ] BULB
- [ ] TREE
- [ ] GRASS
- [ ] EVERGREEN
- [ ] SHRUB
- [ ] FLOWER
- [ ] GROUNDCOVER
- [ ] VINE
- [ ] BERRY
- [ ] ANNUAL
- [ ] PERENNIAL
- [ ] TRANSPLANT
- [ ] BIENNIAL
- [ ] SEED

PURCHASE INFORMATION

VENDOR:

COST:　QTY:

WATERING SCHEDULE

SUNLIGHT EXPOSURE

SOIL REQUIREMENTS

- [ ] ACID
- [ ] ALKALINE

CARE INSTRUCTIONS:

PLANT WORTHINESS:

FERTILIZER/TREATMENTS:

INSECT/DISEASE PROBLEMS:

ADDITIONAL NOTES:

28

COMMON NAME: BOTANICAL NAME:

PLANT VARIETY: DATE PLANTED:

BLOOM SEASON/COLOR: DATE HARVESTED:

- [ ] BULB
- [ ] EVERGREEN
- [ ] GROUNDCOVER
- [ ] ANNUAL
- [ ] BIENNIAL
- [ ] TREE
- [ ] SHRUB
- [ ] VINE
- [ ] PERENNIAL
- [ ] SEED
- [ ] GRASS
- [ ] FLOWER
- [ ] BERRY
- [ ] TRANSPLANT

PURCHASE INFORMATION

VENDOR:

COST: QTY:

WATERING SCHEDULE

SUNLIGHT EXPOSURE

SOIL REQUIREMENTS

- [ ] ACID
- [ ] ALKALINE

CARE INSTRUCTIONS:

PLANT WORTHINESS:

FERTILIZER/TREATMENTS:

INSECT/DISEASE PROBLEMS:

ADDITIONAL NOTES:

29

COMMON NAME: _____   BOTANICAL NAME: _____

PLANT VARIETY: _____

BLOOM SEASON/COLOR: _____

DATE PLANTED: _____

DATE HARVESTED: _____

- ☐ BULB
- ☐ TREE
- ☐ GRASS
- ☐ EVERGREEN
- ☐ SHRUB
- ☐ FLOWER
- ☐ GROUNDCOVER
- ☐ VINE
- ☐ BERRY
- ☐ ANNUAL
- ☐ PERENNIAL
- ☐ TRANSPLANT
- ☐ BIENNIAL
- ☐ SEED

PURCHASE INFORMATION

VENDOR:

COST: QTY:

WATERING SCHEDULE

SUNLIGHT EXPOSURE

SOIL REQUIREMENTS

- ☐ ACID
- ☐ ALKALINE

CARE INSTRUCTIONS:

PLANT WORTHINESS:

FERTILIZER/TREATMENTS:

INSECT/DISEASE PROBLEMS:

ADDITIONAL NOTES:

COMMON NAME: BOTANICAL NAME:

PLANT VARIETY: DATE PLANTED:

BLOOM SEASON/COLOR: DATE HARVESTED:

- [ ] BULB
- [ ] TREE
- [ ] GRASS
- [ ] EVERGREEN
- [ ] SHRUB
- [ ] FLOWER
- [ ] GROUNDCOVER
- [ ] VINE
- [ ] BERRY
- [ ] ANNUAL
- [ ] PERENNIAL
- [ ] TRANSPLANT
- [ ] BIENNIAL
- [ ] SEED

PURCHASE INFORMATION

VENDOR:

COST: QTY:

WATERING SCHEDULE

SUNLIGHT EXPOSURE

SOIL REQUIREMENTS

- [ ] ACID
- [ ] ALKALINE

CARE INSTRUCTIONS:

PLANT WORTHINESS:

FERTILIZER/TREATMENTS:

INSECT/DISEASE PROBLEMS:

ADDITIONAL NOTES:

31

COMMON NAME: BOTANICAL NAME:

PLANT VARIETY: DATE PLANTED:

BLOOM SEASON/COLOR: DATE HARVESTED:

- [ ] BULB   [ ] EVERGREEN   [ ] GROUNDCOVER   [ ] ANNUAL   [ ] BIENNIAL
- [ ] TREE   [ ] SHRUB   [ ] VINE   [ ] PERENNIAL   [ ] SEED
- [ ] GRASS   [ ] FLOWER   [ ] BERRY   [ ] TRANSPLANT

PURCHASE INFORMATION		WATERING SCHEDULE	SOIL REQUIREMENTS
VENDOR:			[ ] ACID
COST:	QTY:	SUNLIGHT EXPOSURE	[ ] ALKALINE

CARE INSTRUCTIONS: PLANT WORTHINESS:

FERTILIZER/TREATMENTS:

INSECT/DISEASE PROBLEMS:

ADDITIONAL NOTES:

32

COMMON NAME: BOTANICAL NAME:

PLANT VARIETY: DATE PLANTED:

BLOOM SEASON/COLOR: DATE HARVESTED:

- [ ] BULB
- [ ] TREE
- [ ] GRASS

- [ ] EVERGREEN
- [ ] SHRUB
- [ ] FLOWER

- [ ] GROUNDCOVER
- [ ] VINE
- [ ] BERRY

- [ ] ANNUAL
- [ ] PERENNIAL
- [ ] TRANSPLANT

- [ ] BIENNIAL
- [ ] SEED

PURCHASE INFORMATION	WATERING SCHEDULE	SOIL REQUIREMENTS
VENDOR:		[ ] ACID
COST: QTY:	SUNLIGHT EXPOSURE	[ ] ALKALINE

CARE INSTRUCTIONS:

PLANT WORTHINESS:

FERTILIZER/TREATMENTS:

INSECT/DISEASE PROBLEMS:

ADDITIONAL NOTES:

33

COMMON NAME:

BOTANICAL NAME:

PLANT VARIETY:

DATE PLANTED:

BLOOM SEASON/COLOR:

DATE HARVESTED:

- [ ] BULB
- [ ] EVERGREEN
- [ ] GROUNDCOVER
- [ ] ANNUAL
- [ ] BIENNIAL
- [ ] TREE
- [ ] SHRUB
- [ ] VINE
- [ ] PERENNIAL
- [ ] SEED
- [ ] GRASS
- [ ] FLOWER
- [ ] BERRY
- [ ] TRANSPLANT

PURCHASE INFORMATION	WATERING SCHEDULE	SOIL REQUIREMENTS
VENDOR:		[ ] ACID
COST: QTY:	SUNLIGHT EXPOSURE	[ ] ALKALINE

CARE INSTRUCTIONS:

PLANT WORTHINESS:

FERTILIZER/TREATMENTS:

INSECT/DISEASE PROBLEMS:

ADDITIONAL NOTES:

COMMON NAME: BOTANICAL NAME:

PLANT VARIETY:

DATE PLANTED:

BLOOM SEASON/COLOR:

DATE HARVESTED:

- ☐ BULB
- ☐ TREE
- ☐ GRASS
- ☐ EVERGREEN
- ☐ SHRUB
- ☐ FLOWER
- ☐ GROUNDCOVER
- ☐ VINE
- ☐ BERRY
- ☐ ANNUAL
- ☐ PERENNIAL
- ☐ TRANSPLANT
- ☐ BIENNIAL
- ☐ SEED

PURCHASE INFORMATION

VENDOR:

COST: QTY:

WATERING SCHEDULE

SUNLIGHT EXPOSURE

SOIL REQUIREMENTS

- ☐ ACID
- ☐ ALKALINE

CARE INSTRUCTIONS:

PLANT WORTHINESS:

FERTILIZER/TREATMENTS:

INSECT/DISEASE PROBLEMS:

ADDITIONAL NOTES:

35

COMMON NAME: | BOTANICAL NAME:

PLANT VARIETY: | DATE PLANTED:

BLOOM SEASON/COLOR: | DATE HARVESTED:

- [ ] BULB
- [ ] EVERGREEN
- [ ] GROUNDCOVER
- [ ] ANNUAL
- [ ] BIENNIAL
- [ ] TREE
- [ ] SHRUB
- [ ] VINE
- [ ] PERENNIAL
- [ ] SEED
- [ ] GRASS
- [ ] FLOWER
- [ ] BERRY
- [ ] TRANSPLANT

PURCHASE INFORMATION

VENDOR:

COST: | QTY:

WATERING SCHEDULE

SUNLIGHT EXPOSURE

SOIL REQUIREMENTS

- [ ] ACID
- [ ] ALKALINE

CARE INSTRUCTIONS:

PLANT WORTHINESS:

FERTILIZER/TREATMENTS:

INSECT/DISEASE PROBLEMS:

ADDITIONAL NOTES:

Sow your seed in the morning,
and at evening let your hands
not be idle, for you do not know
which will succeed, whether
this or that, or whether both
will do equally well.

Ecclesiastes 11:6

Part Four

Seasonal Gardening Tasks

Now that you have designed, planned, and listed items to purchase for your garden, this section is where you'll create a personalized garden plan for yourself that is specific to your growing conditions. Here, you'll find plenty of space to track and record information that is relevant to your flower garden. There's also a handy list of tasks to do in each month or season of your garden to help you stay on top of things and keep your garden beautiful all year long.

Yearly
PLANNING

This section will help you plan your garden for the upcoming year. Include the following overview:

- Your specific first and last frost date (what was predicted vs. what occurred)

- Any unusual weather patterns (hurricanes, excessive heat, drought, etc.) that might affect your garden

- Planting times, germination for seed starting, first and last blooms (read your seed packets to determine when you should start sowing each variety)

- Any large projects you undertook for the season, such as starting a cut flower garden or building raised garden beds

Use these pages to jot down all that's happening in the garden beds, as you'll use it as a reference tool later.

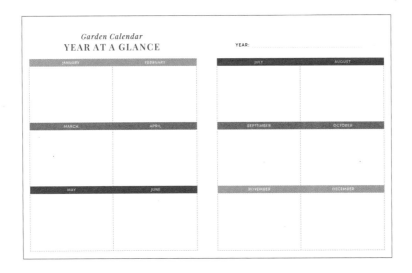

Seasonal/Monthly
PLANNING

This is where you'll record what's happening in the "Seasonal/Monthly Gardening Tasks" (see pages 123-137) to ensure you don't miss anything you wanted to do during the season. I can't tell you how many times I told myself I'd do something, and then completely spaced and forgot all about it until it was too late. This will help you remember and stay on track!

Garden Calendar
MONTH AT A GLANCE

MONTH: _____   YEAR: _____

SUNDAY	MONDAY	TUESDAY	WEDNESDAY	THURSDAY

FRIDAY	SATURDAY

MY MONTHLY TASKS

- ☐ _____
- ☐ _____
- ☐ _____
- ☐ _____
- ☐ _____
- ☐ _____
- ☐ _____
- ☐ _____
- ☐ _____
- ☐ _____
- ☐ _____
- ☐ _____
- ☐ _____
- ☐ _____
- ☐ _____
- ☐ _____
- ☐ _____
- ☐ _____
- ☐ _____

Weekly
PLANNING

Use these pages to create your to-do list and make any other notes about your garden. If you are starting small, you may not use everything in these planning calendars all at once, and that's just fine. The main thing is to get in the habit of keeping notes. The more gardening experience you get, the more you'll learn and be able to journal about:

- Soil tests, amendments, mulching, and fertilizing applications

- Staking and supporting flowers

- Signs of pests and plant disease

- Flowers that are blooming beautifully or flopped

- Seed-starting and sowing dates

- Planting dates

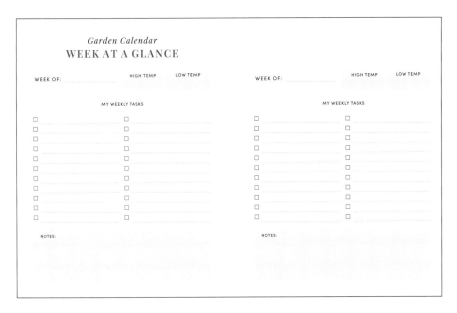

Seasonal/Monthly
GARDENING TASKS

Your gardening zone will dictate what you are doing, planting, and growing in your flower garden. If it's warm enough outdoors for the ground to be worked, you'll be able to work on your garden earlier in the year than someone who's gardening in a colder climate. Keep in mind that these dates are estimated guidelines that will vary from year to year.

Many gardeners call these monthly tasks a "to-do list," but I prefer to look at them seasonally so I can plan and proceed based on how things are going in my specific climate. Every year is different, so think of these as general guidelines.

I realize that the term "gardening tasks" sounds like a lot of work, and it can scare overwhelmed or new gardeners. The truth is, you don't have to do *everything* on the list. Prioritize what you need to do, what you want to do, and what you think should be happening in your garden this year. *Then go with the flow!* These tasks will keep you on track with things you may not think of in the moment and serve as reminders of things you may eventually want to do.

Make sure you use your seed-starting chart to determine precise sowing and planting times. Also keep in mind that this monthly task guide is for an easy-care approach to flower gardening. You can apply many of these same principles to growing other things, and I have included a few helpful hints for your vegetable garden, but I'm gearing these tasks to help you get started on a successful flower-gardening journey. Just keep in mind that what you might find in an average garden planner might look a little different from this one.

Mid-Winter (January-ish)

While the start of the new year is a great time to get organized and excited for the upcoming growing season, it's also okay to take a breather and pace yourself. If you can't wait to dive in, though, there are a few things you can do this month to get your bloom on.

- Dream big as you sketch out your ideas, create mood boards, and design your garden layout, noting practical considerations like the best blooms for your area, sun exposure, and companion plants. Research plants you want to grow, follow gardeners on social media and TV, order plant catalogs, and read gardening magazines. Visit an arboretum or go on a neighborhood walk for inspiration.

- Clean and organize your garden tools, supplies, and garage or outbuildings.

- Inventory seeds you already have on hand so you can plan your seed order.

- Order seeds. Keep in mind that seeds and plants from high-quality and popular growers sell out quickly, so shop early.

- Order bare root plants, tubers, and rhizomes (like bearded iris and roses).

- Check on overwintering plants, tubers, and bulbs (if you brought any indoors).

- Depending on what you are starting from seed, you may start sowing seeds. Start seeds indoors, or try winter sowing outdoors in recycled containers. Shop for seed-starting equipment, such as heat mats and grow lights, for optimal germination. If you're reusing supplies, sanitize cell trays with a 1:10 bleach to water ratio.

- Check your garden supply inventory. Clean and oil tools and sharpen pruners. Update your garden gear, and get your gardening gloves and boots ready for spring action.

- If you want to save money and make your own compost this year, start composting kitchen scraps and start a pile outdoors to help improve your garden soil in the spring.

- If you have a pond with fish, add pond dye to darken the water so predators can't see your precious fish. This keeps them from dining and dashing in the middle of winter when food is scarce.

- Fill bird feeders to keep your feathered friends well-fed in the coldest months.

- Spray deer repellent on evergreen foliage that is susceptible to deer damage.

- Walk your gardens every day to spot issues you may wish to address and to keep an eye on evergreen plants that are susceptible to damage.

Late Winter (February-ish)

The weather may be bleak, but you can still get excited for the upcoming growing season! If you are starting a cut flower garden, you'll be in the thick of starting seeds both indoors and out (if winter sowing). Here are a few other things you can do to get ready for spring:

- Order seeds and plants if you want varieties that aren't available in local nurseries.

- Continue sowing seeds indoors. Follow the seed packet instructions, paying special attention to the sowing date and your last frost date. Label every single pot or cell clearly so you can remember what you planted. (Trust me, you won't always remember!)

- If your climate is temperate enough, add compost and fresh soil to your raised garden beds so they are ready for planting. If it's not too cold out, top-dressing existing garden beds with a light layer of aged manure or compost will do wonders for your garden's health.

- Service garden power tools like mowers, weeders, and blowers.

- On a nice day, get outside, enjoy some fresh air, and tidy things up! Remove fallen leaves, debris, and spent annuals. Cut back ornamental grasses, panicle hydrangeas, and perennials.

- When it's seasonable, prune unruly branches, dangerous limbs, and plants that bloom on new growth.

- If your roses are forming buds, it's okay to prune them.

- Fill bird feeders.

- Start or add to your compost pile.

- To help wake them up from winter dormancy, start fertilizing your houseplants and overwintered plants in pots that you brought indoors.

- Bring the outdoors in. Cut spring-flowering branches like forsythia, witch hazel, dogwood, crabapple, and flowering cherries so you can force the blooms indoors.

- Check on the seedlings you are winter sowing. Don't fret if you don't see any growth yet. Have patience—some take more time than others to germinate.

- Spray deer repellent on evergreen foliage that's particularly susceptible to deer damage.

Early Spring (March-ish)

We are getting closer! If you live in a warmer climate, you may be getting ready to plant cool-season annuals, perennials, shrubs, and trees. If you are in a cooler climate, you can get outside and continue to prepare for planting. Now is a great time to enjoy the outdoors after a long, cold winter.

- As soon as the ground can be worked, do a soil test to see what's lacking in your soil. Send a soil sample to your local county extension service office for testing so you can learn what nutrients (if any) you need to add to your soil to help your garden thrive.

- Prune dormant trees and shrubs like roses and both panicle hydrangeas and smooth hydrangeas. Know what you are growing before you prune!

- Finish cutting back ornamental grasses and perennials and cleaning up the garden beds if you haven't started doing this yet.

- Continue sowing seeds. You'll feel grateful you did all this work later!

- Till or rake the garden beds, breaking up any tough clumps of dirt. Amend the soil with compost.

- If you wrapped evergreens or hydrangeas in burlap to protect them from winter damage, you can remove the burlap now.

- Plant cool-season annuals, perennials, shrubs, and trees if the ground can be worked. Flowers like pansies, ranunculus, and perennials can take the cooler temperatures. Early spring is also a great time to sow (or plant) cool-season vegetables (if you want to grow them), depending on your gardening zone.

- If you didn't apply compost to your beds, add it now.

- Apply a layer of organic mulch like bark chips or shredded leaves before plants begin to mature. It's easier to apply mulch early in the season, plus it conserves moisture, suppresses weeds, and keeps your soil happy.

- Keep an eye on your spring-flowering bulbs. To protect them from being nibbled, start spraying deer repellent on tulips and other emerging foliage that's susceptible to predator damage as they break ground.

- Dig and divide perennials if they are starting to break ground.

- Keep up with deer repellent on susceptible evergreen foliage.

- Walk your gardens every day to watch for any issues.

Mid-Spring (April-ish)

As spring temperatures warm and cool, keep an eye out for frosts or hard freezes. Cool-season annuals and vegetables should be okay, but severe weather can take them out. Have a frost blanket or crop cover handy in case you need to cover things on the fly.

- Harden off indoor seedlings by gradually exposing them to cooler temperatures. You will start doing this two weeks before your last frost date. Refer to seed packet directions to determine when it is safe to plant that particular variety.

- If you have one, start turning your compost pile to get it cooking.

- Prune roses and other shrubs that bloom on old wood before they leaf out. Be careful with macrophylla hydrangeas, though; wait until the plant leafs out before you prune it.

- Plant new perennials and cool-season annuals, including flowers, herbs, and vegetables.

- Dig and divide perennials. Move things around to your liking until you're pleased with how they fit your garden design and match your overall aesthetic.

- As perennials break through the ground, move mulch away from them so they get plenty of sunlight.

- Hand-pull or hoe weeds gently before they take over.

- Deadhead spring-flowering bulbs to keep things looking neat and tidy. Keep the foliage intact until it completely browns out.

- Depending on your last frost date, start transplanting hardened-off seedlings in the garden.

- Order spring-flowering bulbs for fall planting. Yes, it's early, but you'll have more of a variety to choose from if you order online now.

- Mark where your spring-flowering bulbs are if you want to plant more in the same area in the fall. If you don't note where they are, you won't know where they were once the foilage dies back.

- As perennials break through the ground, spray hostas and other susceptible plants to prevent deer damage.

- Walk your gardens every day to watch for any issues as plants begin to grow.

Late Spring (May-ish)

It's go time! When there is no more danger of frost, plant your summer-flowering annuals and warm-season vegetables for a bountiful harvest and lots of blooms. Keep an eye on your gardens, as you'll slowly start to see issues crop up. By addressing these issues early, your garden will keep looking amazing—with minimal effort on your part.

- Plant warm-season annual flowers and vegetables like marigolds, petunias, lantana, tomatoes, peppers, and eggplants. Remember, if you're in zone 6 and below, nights can stay cool, so cover tender plants if frost threatens.

- Add a slow-release fertilizer to your flowering annuals, houseplants, and container gardens to ensure lots of blooms. Only use organic fertilizers on anything edible.

- Plant your favorite herbs like basil, parsley, rosemary, dill, oregano, and thyme for fresh culinary delights. Group them near the kitchen (and a water source) for easy access.

- Direct sow seeds of summer bloomers like zinnias, cosmos, borage, calendula, straw-flowers, and sunflowers in the garden.

- Support plants that will grow about three feet tall and become bloom-heavy. It only takes one rain or wind storm to knock your beautiful plants over.

- Plant fast-growing vines to hide eyesores like garbage bins, air conditioner units, or other unsightly areas. Mandevillas and black-eyed Susan vines are just a few options that are fast-growing and perfect for this very purpose.

- Monitor soil moisture, especially during hot spells. Deep watering encourages strong root growth, unlike frequent shallow sprinkles.

- Pot some pretty summer-flowering annuals in containers, hanging baskets, and window boxes to warm up your outdoor living spaces and create a welcoming entrance to your home.

- Use easy-to-find drip irrigation kits with a timer system on pots, hanging baskets, and window boxes to help keep your watering chores to a minimum. Drip irrigation is the best way to keep those container plants alive in the dog days of summer.

- If you start noticing holes in your plants, look for potential pests on that particular plant before doing anything else.

- If slugs or snails are a problem, apply organic slug and snail bait around plants each month to keep the damage at bay.

- Spray deer repellent on plants that are susceptible to damage.

- Walk your gardens every day to watch for any issues as plants begin to grow.

Early Summer (June-ish)

June is a great time to admire your garden and pat yourself on the back for all the work you've put in. Everything is starting to look gorgeous as plants become established, bloom, and grow. But don't let your guard down; some issues may still crop up as you head into summer.

- Start cutting flowers if there are blooms in your cut flower garden. The more you cut, the more they'll bloom!

- Harvest cool-season veggies, herbs, and anything that's ripe for the picking.

- Pinch back dahlias and seedlings like zinnias, cosmos, and snapdragons to promote branchier growth when they reach about a foot tall. This will help you get even more blooms in your flower garden.

- Set up supports for plants that will get tall and/or bloom-heavy.

- Cut back leggy annuals like petunias and marigolds for bushier growth and more blooms if they start looking straggly.

- Deadhead flowers regularly to promote continuous blooms.

- Pull weeds before they go to seed, minimizing future battles. If necessary, mulch around established plants for extra weed suppression, but leave enough space before the plant base to allow for improved air circulation and avoid too much moisture retention that can cause pest and disease problems.

- Prune shrubs that bloom on old wood immediately after they flower.

- Keep sowing sunflowers and other one-and-done varieties to keep the blooms coming for weeks instead of days.

- Start watching for signs of Japanese beetles—once they arrive, they can decimate your foliage. As soon as you see them, knock them off your plants and into a soapy bucket of water.

- Spray deer repellent on plants that are susceptible to deer damage.

- Walk your gardens every day to watch for problems as plants begin to grow.

Mid-Summer (July-ish)

July is usually the time I start noticing pest and disease issues cropping up in the garden. From pests like Japanese beetles, aphids, slugs, and snails to plant disease like powdery mildew, addressing these issues as they appear will keep any damage to a minimum. Keep in mind there is no one fix to every problem. How you address things will depend on the plant and the issue that is occurring. Remember—do not blindly apply pesticides in your garden!

When it starts to get really hot outside, container gardens will dry out much faster. If you have a drip irrigation system set up, you'll want to run it every day to keep your plants hydrated in excessive heat. Once I got my containers on drip irrigation, they truly flourished during scorching summers—with absolutely no work from me.

- Keep watering consistently, especially during heat waves. Apply a light water-soluble fertilizer to blooming plants for sustained color and blooms.

- Continue to cut back plants that are getting leggy and look straggly.

- Watch for signs of insect pests like aphids and Japanese beetles.

- Deadhead spent flowers. Cut back perennials like salvia and nepeta halfway to encourage a second set of blooms as the first flowers fade.

- Continue to weed. Yes, it's hot out, but don't let things get out of control. Noxious weeds can totally take over your garden and wreck all of your hard work. Go outside in the early morning or evening to keep up with garden chores.

- If you didn't use a slow-release fertilizer for summer-flowering annuals, houseplants, and container gardens, you'll need to keep feeding them with a water-soluble fertilizer.

- Harvest herbs and vegetables regularly.

- Keep cutting flowers, making bouquets and enjoying them indoors and out. This keeps the blooms coming!

- Support plants that are toppling over.

- If you travel for vacation, remember to set up a drip irrigation system or ask a friend to water while you're out of town.

- Spray deer repellent on plants that are susceptible to damage.

- Walk your gardens every day to watch for issues as plants continue to grow.

Late Summer (August-ish)

If your plants are starting to look a little tired, make sure you've kept up with fertilizing them. Cut back leggy growth on trailing annuals and keep deadheading spent flowers. If you used a slow-release fertilizer, you'll likely need to apply another application this month to keep your flowers blooming and happy well into the fall.

- Keep cutting flowers from your cut flower garden daily.

- Support flowers and plants that are toppling over.

- Enjoy the peak of your vegetable bounty! Tomatoes, peppers, eggplants, and beans are all reaching their prime. Preserve your harvest by canning, freezing, or dehydrating.

- Want to save some money next year? Collect seeds from spent blooms of strawflowers, calendula, sunflowers, and zinnias for next year's garden.

- Deadhead fading perennials and cut back spent annuals to encourage new growth and tidy up the beds.

- If the garden beds and containers are looking dull, replace summer-flowering annuals to spruce things up.

- Repot houseplants that are not thriving. They likely need their soil to be refreshed.

- Harvest herbs and vegetables regularly.

- If you are growing roses in the northern part of the country, this is the last month you'll feed them so you can give them time to go into dormancy before winter.

- Resist the temptation to buy chrysanthemums now. It's too early and too hot for them!

- Spray deer repellent on plants that are susceptible to damage.

- Walk your gardens every day to watch for problems.

Early Fall (September-ish)

As we move into fall, the garden starts to wind down. It's time for fall plantings and adding creative touches to gardens and outdoor living spaces to ramp up the autumn aesthetic.

- Start shopping for perennials, shrubs, and trees. They will start going on serious markdown in late September/early October, as nurseries want to sell off their stock before winter. Now is the time to start planting again, so the timing couldn't be better.

- Dig, divide, and transplant perennials as the weather starts to cool. Don't do it when it's hot out. Time this task around a rain if you can, so it will be less watering work for you.

- Keep saving seeds.

- Gather fallen leaves and kitchen scraps to build your own compost and leaf mold piles. It's nature's free fertilizer!

- Clean and store your gardening tools before they hibernate for the winter. Sharpen blades, oil moving parts, and hang them safely in a cool, dry place.

- Harvest herbs and veggies, and keep cutting your flowers.

- Order amaryllis bulbs and paperwhites so you can easily grow flowers indoors during the winter.

- You may start to notice some powdery mildew on plants in September. A result of cooler nights and warmer days, this is a natural part of the plant life cycle. Just leave them be until the end of the growing season, or if they're too unsightly, pull them out or cut them back.

- Swap out summer-flowering annuals that don't look amazing anymore for pansies that will add fall color and bounce back again in the spring. Tuck in ornamental grasses, celosia, and marigolds to ramp up the fall color and texture. If the weather is cooling down, tuck in some garden mums for quick fall color.

- Stop fertilizing plants if you are gardening in a cooler climate.

- Keep your eye out for a frost so you can cover or protect plants.

- Sow cool-season veggies like kale, spinach, and Swiss chard directly in the garden for a delicious autumn harvest.

- Bring in tender container plants before the first frost. Give them a warm, sunny spot indoors and adjust their watering needs.

- Spray deer repellent on plants that are susceptible to damage.

- Walk your gardens every day to watch for any issues.

Mid-Fall (October–ish)

Now's the time to keep an eye out for the first frost if it didn't happen already and to prepare the garden for winter.

- When raking leaves, try shredding them and adding them to your leaf mold and compost piles, or use them as a winter mulch for your garden beds.

- Plant fall-blooming bulbs like crocuses, daffodils, hyacinths, alliums, and tulips for a vibrant spring show.

- If you haven't already, plant garden mums and pansies for fall color.

- Add a layer of mulch around fall-planted bulbs to protect them from harsh winter freezes.

- Cut the last blossoms from your cut flower garden before the first frost, and harvest any vegetables or herbs you've been growing.

- Lift and overwinter tender perennials and bulbs like dahlias, caladiums, colocasia, and canna lilies.

- Drain and store hoses, birdbaths, and fountains to prevent frost damage. Disconnect and store pumps safely. Cover heavy concrete and other non-movable containers to prevent freeze damage.

- Wash out all containers with a 1:10 bleach ratio before storing.

- Clean and sanitize garden tools. Sharpen blades.

- Plant amaryllis bulbs and paperwhites for holiday and winter blooms indoors.

- Start planning for next year! Reflect on your successes and challenges. Update your garden journal with notes for next year's plantings, and order seeds from trusted catalogs.

- Clean out leaves from your garden. Don't allow them to mat down your plants or pile up. Rodents tend to make their homes in piled-up leaves and can do significant damage to plant roots.

- Spray deer repellent on plants that are susceptible to damage. Even evergreens like rhododendrons, azaleas, mountain laurels, and yews are prone to nibbling! Stay vigilant.

- Walk your gardens every day to watch for any issues.

Late Fall (November-ish)

By now, you've likely had your first frost, are putting the garden to rest for the year, and are looking ahead to the holidays.

- It's a good idea to top-dress your entire garden with a generous layer of organic mulch like shredded leaves or bark chips. This will protect your soil and plants from winter's wrath.

- Keep cleaning leaves out of the garden beds. It's okay to keep some, but don't allow them to pile up around your plants, or rodents might make a home there.

- You can still plant spring-flowering bulbs, perennials, shrubs, and trees if the ground can be worked.

- If you want to tidy up your garden for winter, cut back the perennials and pull out the rest of the dead annuals.

- Clean and store empty garden containers, tools, and garden decor.

- Set up and fill bird feeders and provide fresh water to attract feathered friends during the lean winter months.

- If you have a pond with fish in it, add dye to help protect them from predators.

- Now is a great time to add Christmas lights to your property while it's still warm out! It may seem early, but it's much easier to do when the weather is better.

- Spray deer repellent on evergreen plants that are susceptible to damage, such as rhododendrons, azaleas, mountain laurels, and yews.

Early Winter (December-ish)

With the holidays upon us, it's the perfect time for gardeners to take a much-needed break. However, I like to use this time to spruce up outdoor containers with winter greenery and other festive decor. Here are a few things you can do if you want to keep gardening through the winter:

- Add some winter greenery outside your front door and in your window boxes to cozy up planters and make things look festive for the holiday season.

- Make a kissing ball, garlands, wreaths, and centerpieces with fresh winter greens.

- Spray deer repellent on evergreen plants that are susceptible to damage, like rhododendrons, azaleas, mountain laurels, and yews.

- Take some time to dream and plan for next year's garden. Browse seed and plant catalogs, sketch new layouts, and research new plants you might want to add.

- Share your passion for gardening! Give gardening books, tools, or seeds as gifts to your favorite plant pals. Propagate houseplants and give them as gifts.

- Winter is a time for rest and rejuvenation. Take a break from the garden, relax, and recharge your batteries for another year of blooming brilliance!

Remember, this is just a general guide. Adapt these tasks to your specific climate, soil conditions, and personal preferences. Don't be afraid to experiment, learn from your mistakes, and, most importantly, have fun in your garden!

**Remember this: Whoever sows
sparingly will also reap sparingly,
and whoever sows generously
will also reap generously.**

2 Corinthians 9:6

Part Five

Personalized Garden Calendar

Ready to transform your outdoor space? This section will help you personalize your gardens by equipping you with the tools to plan and create your flowering oasis. Here, you'll map your schedule for the major tasks for each month and week and find space to track important details to organize your gardening success story.

Garden Calendar
YEAR AT A GLANCE

JANUARY	FEBRUARY

MARCH	APRIL

MAY	JUNE

YEAR: ....

JULY	AUGUST

SEPTEMBER	OCTOBER

NOVEMBER	DECEMBER

Garden Calendar
MONTH AT A GLANCE

SUNDAY	MONDAY	TUESDAY	WEDNESDAY	THURSDAY

MONTH: .... **YEAR:** ....

FRIDAY	SATURDAY

MY MONTHLY TASKS

- ☐ ....
- ☐ ....
- ☐ ....
- ☐ ....
- ☐ ....
- ☐ ....
- ☐ ....
- ☐ ....
- ☐ ....
- ☐ ....
- ☐ ....
- ☐ ....
- ☐ ....
- ☐ ....
- ☐ ....
- ☐ ....
- ☐ ....
- ☐ ....
- ☐ ....
- ☐ ....

Garden Calendar
WEEK AT A GLANCE

WEEK OF: _____   HIGH TEMP   LOW TEMP

MY WEEKLY TASKS

- ☐ ....
- ☐ ....
- ☐ ....
- ☐ ....
- ☐ ....
- ☐ ....
- ☐ ....
- ☐ ....
- ☐ ....
- ☐ ....
- ☐ ....

- ☐ ....
- ☐ ....
- ☐ ....
- ☐ ....
- ☐ ....
- ☐ ....
- ☐ ....
- ☐ ....
- ☐ ....
- ☐ ....
- ☐ ....

NOTES:

WEEK OF: _____   HIGH TEMP   LOW TEMP

MY WEEKLY TASKS

- [ ] _____
- [ ] _____
- [ ] _____
- [ ] _____
- [ ] _____
- [ ] _____
- [ ] _____
- [ ] _____
- [ ] _____
- [ ] _____
- [ ] _____

- [ ] _____
- [ ] _____
- [ ] _____
- [ ] _____
- [ ] _____
- [ ] _____
- [ ] _____
- [ ] _____
- [ ] _____
- [ ] _____
- [ ] _____

NOTES:

Garden Calendar
WEEK AT A GLANCE

WEEK OF: ....

HIGH TEMP

LOW TEMP

MY WEEKLY TASKS

☐ ....
☐ ....
☐ ....
☐ ....
☐ ....
☐ ....
☐ ....
☐ ....
☐ ....
☐ ....
☐ ....

☐ ....
☐ ....
☐ ....
☐ ....
☐ ....
☐ ....
☐ ....
☐ ....
☐ ....
☐ ....
☐ ....

NOTES:

WEEK OF: _____

HIGH TEMP   LOW TEMP

MY WEEKLY TASKS

- [ ] ....
- [ ] ....
- [ ] ....
- [ ] ....
- [ ] ....
- [ ] ....
- [ ] ....
- [ ] ....
- [ ] ....
- [ ] ....
- [ ] ....
- [ ] ....
- [ ] ....

NOTES:

WEEK OF: _____

HIGH TEMP   LOW TEMP

MY WEEKLY TASKS

- [ ] ....
- [ ] ....
- [ ] ....
- [ ] ....
- [ ] ....
- [ ] ....
- [ ] ....
- [ ] ....
- [ ] ....
- [ ] ....
- [ ] ....
- [ ] ....
- [ ] ....

NOTES:

Garden Calendar
MONTH AT A GLANCE

SUNDAY	MONDAY	TUESDAY	WEDNESDAY	THURSDAY

MONTH: .... **YEAR:** ....

FRIDAY	SATURDAY

MY MONTHLY TASKS

- ☐ ....
- ☐ ....
- ☐ ....
- ☐ ....
- ☐ ....
- ☐ ....
- ☐ ....
- ☐ ....
- ☐ ....
- ☐ ....
- ☐ ....
- ☐ ....
- ☐ ....
- ☐ ....
- ☐ ....
- ☐ ....
- ☐ ....
- ☐ ....
- ☐ ....
- ☐ ....

Garden Calendar
WEEK AT A GLANCE

WEEK OF: _____

HIGH TEMP   LOW TEMP

MY WEEKLY TASKS

☐ ....   ☐ ....
☐ ....   ☐ ....
☐ ....   ☐ ....
☐ ....   ☐ ....
☐ ....   ☐ ....
☐ ....   ☐ ....
☐ ....   ☐ ....
☐ ....   ☐ ....
☐ ....   ☐ ....
☐ ....   ☐ ....
☐ ....   ☐ ....

NOTES:

WEEK OF: _____

HIGH TEMP

LOW TEMP

MY WEEKLY TASKS

☐ ....
☐ ....
☐ ....
☐ ....
☐ ....
☐ ....
☐ ....
☐ ....
☐ ....
☐ ....
☐ ....

☐ ....
☐ ....
☐ ....
☐ ....
☐ ....
☐ ....
☐ ....
☐ ....
☐ ....
☐ ....
☐ ....

NOTES:

Garden Calendar
WEEK AT A GLANCE

WEEK OF: ....

HIGH TEMP   LOW TEMP

MY WEEKLY TASKS

- ☐ ....
- ☐ ....
- ☐ ....
- ☐ ....
- ☐ ....
- ☐ ....
- ☐ ....
- ☐ ....
- ☐ ....
- ☐ ....
- ☐ ....

- ☐ ....
- ☐ ....
- ☐ ....
- ☐ ....
- ☐ ....
- ☐ ....
- ☐ ....
- ☐ ....
- ☐ ....
- ☐ ....
- ☐ ....

NOTES:

WEEK OF: _____

HIGH TEMP   LOW TEMP

MY WEEKLY TASKS

- ☐ ....
- ☐ ....
- ☐ ....
- ☐ ....
- ☐ ....
- ☐ ....
- ☐ ....
- ☐ ....
- ☐ ....
- ☐ ....
- ☐ ....
- ☐ ....
- ☐ ....

NOTES:

WEEK OF: _____

HIGH TEMP   LOW TEMP

MY WEEKLY TASKS

- ☐ ....
- ☐ ....
- ☐ ....
- ☐ ....
- ☐ ....
- ☐ ....
- ☐ ....
- ☐ ....
- ☐ ....
- ☐ ....
- ☐ ....
- ☐ ....
- ☐ ....

NOTES:

Garden Calendar
MONTH AT A GLANCE

SUNDAY	MONDAY	TUESDAY	WEDNESDAY	THURSDAY

MONTH: _____ YEAR: _____

FRIDAY	SATURDAY

MY MONTHLY TASKS

☐ ....
☐ ....
☐ ....
☐ ....
☐ ....
☐ ....
☐ ....
☐ ....
☐ ....
☐ ....
☐ ....
☐ ....
☐ ....
☐ ....
☐ ....
☐ ....
☐ ....
☐ ....
☐ ....
☐ ....

Garden Calendar
WEEK AT A GLANCE

WEEK OF: .... HIGH TEMP   LOW TEMP

MY WEEKLY TASKS

☐ ....   ☐ ....
☐ ....   ☐ ....
☐ ....   ☐ ....
☐ ....   ☐ ....
☐ ....   ☐ ....
☐ ....   ☐ ....
☐ ....   ☐ ....
☐ ....   ☐ ....
☐ ....   ☐ ....
☐ ....   ☐ ....
☐ ....   ☐ ....

NOTES:

WEEK OF: _____   HIGH TEMP   LOW TEMP

MY WEEKLY TASKS

- [ ] ....
- [ ] ....
- [ ] ....
- [ ] ....
- [ ] ....
- [ ] ....
- [ ] ....
- [ ] ....
- [ ] ....
- [ ] ....
- [ ] ....

- [ ] ....
- [ ] ....
- [ ] ....
- [ ] ....
- [ ] ....
- [ ] ....
- [ ] ....
- [ ] ....
- [ ] ....
- [ ] ....
- [ ] ....

NOTES:

Garden Calendar
WEEK AT A GLANCE

WEEK OF: _____

HIGH TEMP   LOW TEMP

MY WEEKLY TASKS

- ☐ ....
- ☐ ....
- ☐ ....
- ☐ ....
- ☐ ....
- ☐ ....
- ☐ ....
- ☐ ....
- ☐ ....
- ☐ ....
- ☐ ....

- ☐ ....
- ☐ ....
- ☐ ....
- ☐ ....
- ☐ ....
- ☐ ....
- ☐ ....
- ☐ ....
- ☐ ....
- ☐ ....
- ☐ ....

NOTES:

WEEK OF: _____

HIGH TEMP   LOW TEMP

MY WEEKLY TASKS

- ☐ _____
- ☐ _____
- ☐ _____
- ☐ _____
- ☐ _____
- ☐ _____
- ☐ _____
- ☐ _____
- ☐ _____
- ☐ _____
- ☐ _____
- ☐ _____
- ☐ _____

NOTES:

WEEK OF: _____

HIGH TEMP   LOW TEMP

MY WEEKLY TASKS

- ☐ _____
- ☐ _____
- ☐ _____
- ☐ _____
- ☐ _____
- ☐ _____
- ☐ _____
- ☐ _____
- ☐ _____
- ☐ _____
- ☐ _____
- ☐ _____
- ☐ _____

NOTES:

Garden Calendar
MONTH AT A GLANCE

SUNDAY	MONDAY	TUESDAY	WEDNESDAY	THURSDAY

MONTH: ....

YEAR: ....

FRIDAY	SATURDAY

MY MONTHLY TASKS

☐ ....
☐ ....
☐ ....
☐ ....
☐ ....
☐ ....
☐ ....
☐ ....
☐ ....
☐ ....
☐ ....
☐ ....
☐ ....
☐ ....
☐ ....
☐ ....
☐ ....
☐ ....
☐ ....
☐ ....

Garden Calendar
WEEK AT A GLANCE

WEEK OF: _____   HIGH TEMP   LOW TEMP

MY WEEKLY TASKS

- ☐ ....
- ☐ ....
- ☐ ....
- ☐ ....
- ☐ ....
- ☐ ....
- ☐ ....
- ☐ ....
- ☐ ....
- ☐ ....
- ☐ ....

- ☐ ....
- ☐ ....
- ☐ ....
- ☐ ....
- ☐ ....
- ☐ ....
- ☐ ....
- ☐ ....
- ☐ ....
- ☐ ....
- ☐ ....

NOTES:

WEEK OF: ....   HIGH TEMP   LOW TEMP

MY WEEKLY TASKS

☐ ....   ☐ ....
☐ ....   ☐ ....
☐ ....   ☐ ....
☐ ....   ☐ ....
☐ ....   ☐ ....
☐ ....   ☐ ....
☐ ....   ☐ ....
☐ ....   ☐ ....
☐ ....   ☐ ....
☐ ....   ☐ ....
☐ ....   ☐ ....

NOTES:

Garden Calendar
WEEK AT A GLANCE

WEEK OF: _____   HIGH TEMP   LOW TEMP

MY WEEKLY TASKS

☐ ....   ☐ ....
☐ ....   ☐ ....
☐ ....   ☐ ....
☐ ....   ☐ ....
☐ ....   ☐ ....
☐ ....   ☐ ....
☐ ....   ☐ ....
☐ ....   ☐ ....
☐ ....   ☐ ....
☐ ....   ☐ ....
☐ ....   ☐ ....

NOTES:

WEEK OF: _____

HIGH TEMP   LOW TEMP

MY WEEKLY TASKS

☐ ....
☐ ....
☐ ....
☐ ....
☐ ....
☐ ....
☐ ....
☐ ....
☐ ....
☐ ....
☐ ....
☐ ....
☐ ....

NOTES:

WEEK OF: _____

HIGH TEMP   LOW TEMP

MY WEEKLY TASKS

☐ ....
☐ ....
☐ ....
☐ ....
☐ ....
☐ ....
☐ ....
☐ ....
☐ ....
☐ ....
☐ ....
☐ ....
☐ ....

NOTES:

Garden Calendar
MONTH AT A GLANCE

SUNDAY	MONDAY	TUESDAY	WEDNESDAY	THURSDAY

MONTH: _____　　**YEAR:** _____

FRIDAY	SATURDAY

MY MONTHLY TASKS

- ☐ _____
- ☐ _____
- ☐ _____
- ☐ _____
- ☐ _____
- ☐ _____
- ☐ _____
- ☐ _____
- ☐ _____
- ☐ _____
- ☐ _____
- ☐ _____
- ☐ _____
- ☐ _____
- ☐ _____
- ☐ _____
- ☐ _____
- ☐ _____
- ☐ _____
- ☐ _____

Garden Calendar
WEEK AT A GLANCE

WEEK OF: _____   HIGH TEMP   LOW TEMP

MY WEEKLY TASKS

- [ ] ....
- [ ] ....
- [ ] ....
- [ ] ....
- [ ] ....
- [ ] ....
- [ ] ....
- [ ] ....
- [ ] ....
- [ ] ....
- [ ] ....

- [ ] ....
- [ ] ....
- [ ] ....
- [ ] ....
- [ ] ....
- [ ] ....
- [ ] ....
- [ ] ....
- [ ] ....
- [ ] ....
- [ ] ....

NOTES:

WEEK OF: ....

HIGH TEMP   LOW TEMP

MY WEEKLY TASKS

- [ ] ....
- [ ] ....
- [ ] ....
- [ ] ....
- [ ] ....
- [ ] ....
- [ ] ....
- [ ] ....
- [ ] ....
- [ ] ....
- [ ] ....

- [ ] ....
- [ ] ....
- [ ] ....
- [ ] ....
- [ ] ....
- [ ] ....
- [ ] ....
- [ ] ....
- [ ] ....
- [ ] ....
- [ ] ....

NOTES:

Garden Calendar
WEEK AT A GLANCE

WEEK OF: _____   HIGH TEMP   LOW TEMP

MY WEEKLY TASKS

- [ ] ....
- [ ] ....
- [ ] ....
- [ ] ....
- [ ] ....
- [ ] ....
- [ ] ....
- [ ] ....
- [ ] ....
- [ ] ....
- [ ] ....

- [ ] ....
- [ ] ....
- [ ] ....
- [ ] ....
- [ ] ....
- [ ] ....
- [ ] ....
- [ ] ....
- [ ] ....
- [ ] ....
- [ ] ....

NOTES:

WEEK OF: _____

HIGH TEMP

LOW TEMP

MY WEEKLY TASKS

- [ ] _____
- [ ] _____
- [ ] _____
- [ ] _____
- [ ] _____
- [ ] _____
- [ ] _____
- [ ] _____
- [ ] _____
- [ ] _____
- [ ] _____
- [ ] _____
- [ ] _____

NOTES:

WEEK OF: _____

HIGH TEMP

LOW TEMP

MY WEEKLY TASKS

- [ ] _____
- [ ] _____
- [ ] _____
- [ ] _____
- [ ] _____
- [ ] _____
- [ ] _____
- [ ] _____
- [ ] _____
- [ ] _____
- [ ] _____
- [ ] _____
- [ ] _____

NOTES:

MONTH AT A GLANCE

SUNDAY	MONDAY	TUESDAY	WEDNESDAY	THURSDAY

MONTH: _____   YEAR: _____

FRIDAY	SATURDAY

MY MONTHLY TASKS

- ☐ ....
- ☐ ....
- ☐ ....
- ☐ ....
- ☐ ....
- ☐ ....
- ☐ ....
- ☐ ....
- ☐ ....
- ☐ ....
- ☐ ....
- ☐ ....
- ☐ ....
- ☐ ....
- ☐ ....
- ☐ ....
- ☐ ....
- ☐ ....

Garden Calendar
WEEK AT A GLANCE

WEEK OF: _____   HIGH TEMP   LOW TEMP

MY WEEKLY TASKS

☐ ....   ☐ ....

☐ ....   ☐ ....

☐ ....   ☐ ....

☐ ....   ☐ ....

☐ ....   ☐ ....

☐ ....   ☐ ....

☐ ....   ☐ ....

☐ ....   ☐ ....

☐ ....   ☐ ....

☐ ....   ☐ ....

☐ ....   ☐ ....

NOTES:

WEEK OF: _____

HIGH TEMP   LOW TEMP

MY WEEKLY TASKS

☐ ....   ☐ ....
☐ ....   ☐ ....
☐ ....   ☐ ....
☐ ....   ☐ ....
☐ ....   ☐ ....
☐ ....   ☐ ....
☐ ....   ☐ ....
☐ ....   ☐ ....
☐ ....   ☐ ....
☐ ....   ☐ ....
☐ ....   ☐ ....

NOTES:

Garden Calendar
WEEK AT A GLANCE

WEEK OF: _____   HIGH TEMP   LOW TEMP

MY WEEKLY TASKS

- ☐ ....
- ☐ ....
- ☐ ....
- ☐ ....
- ☐ ....
- ☐ ....
- ☐ ....
- ☐ ....
- ☐ ....
- ☐ ....
- ☐ ....

- ☐ ....
- ☐ ....
- ☐ ....
- ☐ ....
- ☐ ....
- ☐ ....
- ☐ ....
- ☐ ....
- ☐ ....
- ☐ ....
- ☐ ....

NOTES:

WEEK OF: _____

HIGH TEMP   LOW TEMP

MY WEEKLY TASKS

- [ ] _____
- [ ] _____
- [ ] _____
- [ ] _____
- [ ] _____
- [ ] _____
- [ ] _____
- [ ] _____
- [ ] _____
- [ ] _____
- [ ] _____
- [ ] _____
- [ ] _____

NOTES:

WEEK OF: _____

HIGH TEMP   LOW TEMP

MY WEEKLY TASKS

- [ ] _____
- [ ] _____
- [ ] _____
- [ ] _____
- [ ] _____
- [ ] _____
- [ ] _____
- [ ] _____
- [ ] _____
- [ ] _____
- [ ] _____
- [ ] _____
- [ ] _____

NOTES:

Garden Calendar
MONTH AT A GLANCE

SUNDAY	MONDAY	TUESDAY	WEDNESDAY	THURSDAY

MONTH: .... YEAR: ....

FRIDAY	SATURDAY

MY MONTHLY TASKS

- ☐ ....
- ☐ ....
- ☐ ....
- ☐ ....
- ☐ ....
- ☐ ....
- ☐ ....
- ☐ ....
- ☐ ....
- ☐ ....
- ☐ ....
- ☐ ....
- ☐ ....
- ☐ ....
- ☐ ....
- ☐ ....
- ☐ ....
- ☐ ....
- ☐ ....
- ☐ ....

Garden Calendar

WEEK AT A GLANCE

WEEK OF: _____   HIGH TEMP   LOW TEMP

MY WEEKLY TASKS

☐ ....   ☐ ....
☐ ....   ☐ ....
☐ ....   ☐ ....
☐ ....   ☐ ....
☐ ....   ☐ ....
☐ ....   ☐ ....
☐ ....   ☐ ....
☐ ....   ☐ ....
☐ ....   ☐ ....
☐ ....   ☐ ....
☐ ....   ☐ ....

NOTES:

WEEK OF: _____   HIGH TEMP   LOW TEMP

MY WEEKLY TASKS

☐ ....   ☐ ....
☐ ....   ☐ ....
☐ ....   ☐ ....
☐ ....   ☐ ....
☐ ....   ☐ ....
☐ ....   ☐ ....
☐ ....   ☐ ....
☐ ....   ☐ ....
☐ ....   ☐ ....
☐ ....   ☐ ....
☐ ....   ☐ ....

NOTES:

Garden Calendar
WEEK AT A GLANCE

WEEK OF: _____

HIGH TEMP   LOW TEMP

MY WEEKLY TASKS

- ☐ ....
- ☐ ....
- ☐ ....
- ☐ ....
- ☐ ....
- ☐ ....
- ☐ ....
- ☐ ....
- ☐ ....
- ☐ ....
- ☐ ....

- ☐ ....
- ☐ ....
- ☐ ....
- ☐ ....
- ☐ ....
- ☐ ....
- ☐ ....
- ☐ ....
- ☐ ....
- ☐ ....
- ☐ ....

NOTES:

WEEK OF: _____

HIGH TEMP   LOW TEMP

MY WEEKLY TASKS

- [ ]
- [ ]
- [ ]
- [ ]
- [ ]
- [ ]
- [ ]
- [ ]
- [ ]
- [ ]
- [ ]
- [ ]
- [ ]

NOTES:

WEEK OF: _____

HIGH TEMP   LOW TEMP

MY WEEKLY TASKS

- [ ]
- [ ]
- [ ]
- [ ]
- [ ]
- [ ]
- [ ]
- [ ]
- [ ]
- [ ]
- [ ]
- [ ]
- [ ]

NOTES:

Garden Calendar
MONTH AT A GLANCE

SUNDAY	MONDAY	TUESDAY	WEDNESDAY	THURSDAY

MONTH: ....   **YEAR:** ....

FRIDAY	SATURDAY

MY MONTHLY TASKS

☐ ....
☐ ....
☐ ....
☐ ....
☐ ....
☐ ....
☐ ....
☐ ....
☐ ....
☐ ....
☐ ....
☐ ....
☐ ....
☐ ....
☐ ....
☐ ....
☐ ....
☐ ....
☐ ....
☐ ....

Garden Calendar
WEEK AT A GLANCE

WEEK OF: _____

HIGH TEMP   LOW TEMP

MY WEEKLY TASKS

☐ ....   ☐ ....
☐ ....   ☐ ....
☐ ....   ☐ ....
☐ ....   ☐ ....
☐ ....   ☐ ....
☐ ....   ☐ ....
☐ ....   ☐ ....
☐ ....   ☐ ....
☐ ....   ☐ ....
☐ ....   ☐ ....
☐ ....   ☐ ....

NOTES:

WEEK OF: _____

HIGH TEMP   LOW TEMP

MY WEEKLY TASKS

☐ ....   ☐ ....
☐ ....   ☐ ....
☐ ....   ☐ ....
☐ ....   ☐ ....
☐ ....   ☐ ....
☐ ....   ☐ ....
☐ ....   ☐ ....
☐ ....   ☐ ....
☐ ....   ☐ ....
☐ ....   ☐ ....
☐ ....   ☐ ....

NOTES:

Garden Calendar
WEEK AT A GLANCE

WEEK OF: ....

HIGH TEMP   LOW TEMP

MY WEEKLY TASKS

☐ ....   ☐ ....

☐ ....   ☐ ....

☐ ....   ☐ ....

☐ ....   ☐ ....

☐ ....   ☐ ....

☐ ....   ☐ ....

☐ ....   ☐ ....

☐ ....   ☐ ....

☐ ....   ☐ ....

☐ ....   ☐ ....

☐ ....   ☐ ....

NOTES:

WEEK OF: _____

HIGH TEMP   LOW TEMP

MY WEEKLY TASKS

- ☐ ....
- ☐ ....
- ☐ ....
- ☐ ....
- ☐ ....
- ☐ ....
- ☐ ....
- ☐ ....
- ☐ ....
- ☐ ....
- ☐ ....
- ☐ ....
- ☐ ....

NOTES:

WEEK OF: _____

HIGH TEMP   LOW TEMP

MY WEEKLY TASKS

- ☐ ....
- ☐ ....
- ☐ ....
- ☐ ....
- ☐ ....
- ☐ ....
- ☐ ....
- ☐ ....
- ☐ ....
- ☐ ....
- ☐ ....
- ☐ ....
- ☐ ....

NOTES:

Garden Calendar
MONTH AT A GLANCE

SUNDAY	MONDAY	TUESDAY	WEDNESDAY	THURSDAY

MONTH: _____   **YEAR:** _____

FRIDAY	SATURDAY

MY MONTHLY TASKS

☐ ....
☐ ....
☐ ....
☐ ....
☐ ....
☐ ....
☐ ....
☐ ....
☐ ....
☐ ....
☐ ....
☐ ....
☐ ....
☐ ....
☐ ....
☐ ....
☐ ....
☐ ....
☐ ....
☐ ....

Garden Calendar
WEEK AT A GLANCE

WEEK OF: _____   HIGH TEMP   LOW TEMP

MY WEEKLY TASKS

- [ ] ....
- [ ] ....
- [ ] ....
- [ ] ....
- [ ] ....
- [ ] ....
- [ ] ....
- [ ] ....
- [ ] ....
- [ ] ....
- [ ] ....

- [ ] ....
- [ ] ....
- [ ] ....
- [ ] ....
- [ ] ....
- [ ] ....
- [ ] ....
- [ ] ....
- [ ] ....
- [ ] ....
- [ ] ....

NOTES:

WEEK OF: _____

<table>
<tr><td>HIGH TEMP</td><td>LOW TEMP</td></tr>
</table>

MY WEEKLY TASKS

- ☐ ....
- ☐ ....
- ☐ ....
- ☐ ....
- ☐ ....
- ☐ ....
- ☐ ....
- ☐ ....
- ☐ ....
- ☐ ....
- ☐ ....

- ☐ ....
- ☐ ....
- ☐ ....
- ☐ ....
- ☐ ....
- ☐ ....
- ☐ ....
- ☐ ....
- ☐ ....
- ☐ ....
- ☐ ....

NOTES:

Garden Calendar
WEEK AT A GLANCE

WEEK OF: _____   HIGH TEMP   LOW TEMP

MY WEEKLY TASKS

- [ ] ....
- [ ] ....
- [ ] ....
- [ ] ....
- [ ] ....
- [ ] ....
- [ ] ....
- [ ] ....
- [ ] ....
- [ ] ....
- [ ] ....

- [ ] ....
- [ ] ....
- [ ] ....
- [ ] ....
- [ ] ....
- [ ] ....
- [ ] ....
- [ ] ....
- [ ] ....
- [ ] ....
- [ ] ....

NOTES:

WEEK OF: _____

HIGH TEMP   LOW TEMP

MY WEEKLY TASKS

- [ ] ....
- [ ] ....
- [ ] ....
- [ ] ....
- [ ] ....
- [ ] ....
- [ ] ....
- [ ] ....
- [ ] ....
- [ ] ....
- [ ] ....
- [ ] ....
- [ ] ....

NOTES:

WEEK OF: _____

HIGH TEMP   LOW TEMP

MY WEEKLY TASKS

- [ ] ....
- [ ] ....
- [ ] ....
- [ ] ....
- [ ] ....
- [ ] ....
- [ ] ....
- [ ] ....
- [ ] ....
- [ ] ....
- [ ] ....
- [ ] ....
- [ ] ....

NOTES:

Garden Calendar
MONTH AT A GLANCE

SUNDAY	MONDAY	TUESDAY	WEDNESDAY	THURSDAY

MONTH: _____ **YEAR:** _____

FRIDAY	SATURDAY

MY MONTHLY TASKS

☐ ....
☐ ....
☐ ....
☐ ....
☐ ....
☐ ....
☐ ....
☐ ....
☐ ....
☐ ....
☐ ....
☐ ....
☐ ....
☐ ....
☐ ....
☐ ....
☐ ....
☐ ....
☐ ....

Garden Calendar
WEEK AT A GLANCE

WEEK OF: _____   HIGH TEMP   LOW TEMP

MY WEEKLY TASKS

☐ ....   ☐ ....

☐ ....   ☐ ....

☐ ....   ☐ ....

☐ ....   ☐ ....

☐ ....   ☐ ....

☐ ....   ☐ ....

☐ ....   ☐ ....

☐ ....   ☐ ....

☐ ....   ☐ ....

☐ ....   ☐ ....

☐ ....   ☐ ....

NOTES:

WEEK OF: _____

HIGH TEMP   LOW TEMP

MY WEEKLY TASKS

☐ ....   ☐ ....
☐ ....   ☐ ....
☐ ....   ☐ ....
☐ ....   ☐ ....
☐ ....   ☐ ....
☐ ....   ☐ ....
☐ ....   ☐ ....
☐ ....   ☐ ....
☐ ....   ☐ ....
☐ ....   ☐ ....
☐ ....   ☐ ....

NOTES:

Garden Calendar
WEEK AT A GLANCE

WEEK OF: ....

HIGH TEMP   LOW TEMP

MY WEEKLY TASKS

☐ ....
☐ ....
☐ ....
☐ ....
☐ ....
☐ ....
☐ ....
☐ ....
☐ ....
☐ ....
☐ ....

☐ ....
☐ ....
☐ ....
☐ ....
☐ ....
☐ ....
☐ ....
☐ ....
☐ ....
☐ ....
☐ ....

NOTES:

WEEK OF: _____

HIGH TEMP	LOW TEMP

MY WEEKLY TASKS

- [ ] ....
- [ ] ....
- [ ] ....
- [ ] ....
- [ ] ....
- [ ] ....
- [ ] ....
- [ ] ....
- [ ] ....
- [ ] ....
- [ ] ....
- [ ] ....

NOTES:

WEEK OF: _____

HIGH TEMP	LOW TEMP

MY WEEKLY TASKS

- [ ] ....
- [ ] ....
- [ ] ....
- [ ] ....
- [ ] ....
- [ ] ....
- [ ] ....
- [ ] ....
- [ ] ....
- [ ] ....
- [ ] ....
- [ ] ....

NOTES:

Garden Calendar
MONTH AT A GLANCE

SUNDAY	MONDAY	TUESDAY	WEDNESDAY	THURSDAY

MONTH: _____   **YEAR:** _____

FRIDAY	SATURDAY

MY MONTHLY TASKS

- ☐ ....
- ☐ ....
- ☐ ....
- ☐ ....
- ☐ ....
- ☐ ....
- ☐ ....
- ☐ ....
- ☐ ....
- ☐ ....
- ☐ ....
- ☐ ....
- ☐ ....
- ☐ ....
- ☐ ....
- ☐ ....
- ☐ ....
- ☐ ....
- ☐ ....
- ☐ ....

WEEK AT A GLANCE

WEEK OF: _____   HIGH TEMP   LOW TEMP

MY WEEKLY TASKS

☐ ....   ☐ ....

☐ ....   ☐ ....

☐ ....   ☐ ....

☐ ....   ☐ ....

☐ ....   ☐ ....

☐ ....   ☐ ....

☐ ....   ☐ ....

☐ ....   ☐ ....

☐ ....   ☐ ....

☐ ....   ☐ ....

☐ ....   ☐ ....

NOTES:

WEEK OF: _____

HIGH TEMP   LOW TEMP

MY WEEKLY TASKS

- ☐ ....
- ☐ ....
- ☐ ....
- ☐ ....
- ☐ ....
- ☐ ....
- ☐ ....
- ☐ ....
- ☐ ....
- ☐ ....
- ☐ ....

- ☐ ....
- ☐ ....
- ☐ ....
- ☐ ....
- ☐ ....
- ☐ ....
- ☐ ....
- ☐ ....
- ☐ ....
- ☐ ....
- ☐ ....

NOTES:

Garden Calendar
WEEK AT A GLANCE

WEEK OF: _____   HIGH TEMP   LOW TEMP

MY WEEKLY TASKS

- ☐ ....
- ☐ ....
- ☐ ....
- ☐ ....
- ☐ ....
- ☐ ....
- ☐ ....
- ☐ ....
- ☐ ....
- ☐ ....
- ☐ ....

- ☐ ....
- ☐ ....
- ☐ ....
- ☐ ....
- ☐ ....
- ☐ ....
- ☐ ....
- ☐ ....
- ☐ ....
- ☐ ....
- ☐ ....

NOTES:

WEEK OF: _____

WEEK OF: _____

HIGH TEMP   LOW TEMP

HIGH TEMP   LOW TEMP

MY WEEKLY TASKS

MY WEEKLY TASKS

- [ ] _____
- [ ] _____
- [ ] _____
- [ ] _____
- [ ] _____
- [ ] _____
- [ ] _____
- [ ] _____
- [ ] _____
- [ ] _____
- [ ] _____
- [ ] _____
- [ ] _____

- [ ] _____
- [ ] _____
- [ ] _____
- [ ] _____
- [ ] _____
- [ ] _____
- [ ] _____
- [ ] _____
- [ ] _____
- [ ] _____
- [ ] _____
- [ ] _____
- [ ] _____

NOTES:

NOTES:

Garden Calendar
MONTH AT A GLANCE

SUNDAY	MONDAY	TUESDAY	WEDNESDAY	THURSDAY

MONTH: ....   **YEAR:** ....

FRIDAY	SATURDAY

MY MONTHLY TASKS

- ☐ ....
- ☐ ....
- ☐ ....
- ☐ ....
- ☐ ....
- ☐ ....
- ☐ ....
- ☐ ....
- ☐ ....
- ☐ ....
- ☐ ....
- ☐ ....
- ☐ ....
- ☐ ....
- ☐ ....
- ☐ ....
- ☐ ....
- ☐ ....
- ☐ ....
- ☐ ....

Garden Calendar
WEEK AT A GLANCE

WEEK OF: _____

HIGH TEMP   LOW TEMP

MY WEEKLY TASKS

☐ ....   ☐ ....

☐ ....   ☐ ....

☐ ....   ☐ ....

☐ ....   ☐ ....

☐ ....   ☐ ....

☐ ....   ☐ ....

☐ ....   ☐ ....

☐ ....   ☐ ....

☐ ....   ☐ ....

☐ ....   ☐ ....

☐ ....   ☐ ....

NOTES:

WEEK OF: ....   HIGH TEMP   LOW TEMP

MY WEEKLY TASKS

☐ ....
☐ ....
☐ ....
☐ ....
☐ ....
☐ ....
☐ ....
☐ ....
☐ ....
☐ ....
☐ ....

☐ ....
☐ ....
☐ ....
☐ ....
☐ ....
☐ ....
☐ ....
☐ ....
☐ ....
☐ ....
☐ ....

NOTES:

Garden Calendar
WEEK AT A GLANCE

WEEK OF: _____   HIGH TEMP   LOW TEMP

MY WEEKLY TASKS

☐ ....   ☐ ....
☐ ....   ☐ ....
☐ ....   ☐ ....
☐ ....   ☐ ....
☐ ....   ☐ ....
☐ ....   ☐ ....
☐ ....   ☐ ....
☐ ....   ☐ ....
☐ ....   ☐ ....
☐ ....   ☐ ....
☐ ....   ☐ ....

NOTES:

WEEK OF: _____

HIGH TEMP   LOW TEMP

MY WEEKLY TASKS

- ☐ ....
- ☐ ....
- ☐ ....
- ☐ ....
- ☐ ....
- ☐ ....
- ☐ ....
- ☐ ....
- ☐ ....
- ☐ ....
- ☐ ....
- ☐ ....
- ☐ ....

NOTES:

WEEK OF: _____

HIGH TEMP   LOW TEMP

MY WEEKLY TASKS

- ☐ ....
- ☐ ....
- ☐ ....
- ☐ ....
- ☐ ....
- ☐ ....
- ☐ ....
- ☐ ....
- ☐ ....
- ☐ ....
- ☐ ....
- ☐ ....
- ☐ ....

NOTES:

I made gardens and parks
and planted all kinds of
fruit trees in them. I made
reservoirs to water groves
of flourishing trees.

Ecclesiastes 2:5-6

Part Six

Reviewing Flower
& Plant Performance

These final pages are for tracking how things actually perform in your gardens. What worked well and was a pleasant surprise? What was an unexpected challenge? When were you most delighted with your garden, and when were you most frustrated? Take notes as you go through the year.

Flower & Plant Performance
FOR A GARDEN YEAR

DATE PLANTED	PLANT VARIETY	QTY	STARTED FROM SEED?	PLANT AGAIN?
			Y N	Y N
			Y N	Y N
			Y N	Y N
			Y N	Y N
			Y N	Y N
			Y N	Y N
			Y N	Y N
			Y N	Y N
			Y N	Y N
			Y N	Y N
			Y N	Y N
			Y N	Y N

DATE PLANTED	PLANT VARIETY	QTY	STARTED FROM SEED?	PLANT AGAIN?
			Y N	Y N
			Y N	Y N
			Y N	Y N
			Y N	Y N
			Y N	Y N
			Y N	Y N
			Y N	Y N
			Y N	Y N
			Y N	Y N
			Y N	Y N
			Y N	Y N
			Y N	Y N
			Y N	Y N
			Y N	Y N
			Y N	Y N

DATE PLANTED	PLANT VARIETY	QTY	STARTED FROM SEED?	PLANT AGAIN?
			Y N	Y N
			Y N	Y N
			Y N	Y N
			Y N	Y N
			Y N	Y N
			Y N	Y N
			Y N	Y N
			Y N	Y N
			Y N	Y N
			Y N	Y N
			Y N	Y N
			Y N	Y N
			Y N	Y N
			Y N	Y N
			Y N	Y N

DATE PLANTED	PLANT VARIETY	QTY	STARTED FROM SEED?	PLANT AGAIN?
			Y N	Y N
			Y N	Y N
			Y N	Y N
			Y N	Y N
			Y N	Y N
			Y N	Y N
			Y N	Y N
			Y N	Y N
			Y N	Y N
			Y N	Y N
			Y N	Y N
			Y N	Y N
			Y N	Y N
			Y N	Y N

NOTES

NOTES

NOTES

About the Author

STACY LING is a blogger and master gardener who has been growing flowers and plants for more than 25 years. She found her joy in gardening while pursuing a law degree. After passing the bar exam and working in the tax industry for a few years, Stacy and her husband, Christopher, moved to the New Jersey suburbs, where she developed a deep passion for all things plants and flowers.

Stacy became a master gardener through the Rutgers Cooperative Extension and started her own garden design business as she helped friends and neighbors plant and grow their own gardens.

Stacy started her garden-and-home blog in 2018 and has grown her brand, Bricks 'n Blooms, by regularly sharing gardening, DIY, and home decor content, as well as easy recipes and entertaining ideas.

She appeared in a segment on *LIVE with Kelly and Mark*, as well as on HGTV in an episode of *Househunters*. You can also find her on Bloom TV Network, where she shares tips, tricks, and inspiration. Stacy's gardens have been featured by Garden Design, Proven Winners, *Horticulture* magazine, and *Fine Gardening* magazine, and she was a finalist in the 2022 Cottages and Bungalows Curb Appeal Contest. She has appeared on several podcasts as well.

In fall 2021, Stacy and her husband purchased the home of their dreams in central New Jersey. They and their three daughters moved into an 1850 farmhouse situated on ten acres with expansive gardens, tree sculptures, and statues.

All Scripture verses are taken from the Holy Bible, New International Version®, NIV®. Copyright © 1973, 1978, 1984, 2011 by Biblica, Inc.™ Used with permission of Zondervan. All rights reserved worldwide. www.zondervan.com. The "NIV" and "New International Version" are trademarks registered in the United States Patent and Trademark Office by Biblica, Inc.™

Cover and interior design by Leah Beachy
Cover image and interior graphics © ann_and_pen / AdobeStock

For bulk or special sales, please call 1-800-547-8979.
Email: CustomerService@hhpbooks.com

TEN PEAKS PRESS is a federally registered trademark of The Hawkins Children's LLC. Harvest House Publishers, Inc., is the exclusive licensee of this trademark.

The Bricks 'n Blooms Beautiful and Easy-Care Flower Garden Planner
Copyright © 2025 by Stacy Ling
Published by Ten Peaks Press, an imprint of Harvest House Publishers
Eugene, Oregon 97408

ISBN 978-0-7369-9075-2 (pbk)

Printed in China

24 25 26 27 28 29 30/ RDS / 10 9 8 7 6 5 4 3 2 1